# Not Released Unharmed

## Kidnap Victims

by

Donald L. Smith

authorHOUSE®

*AuthorHouse™*
*1663 Liberty Drive, Suite 200*
*Bloomington, IN 47403*
*www.authorhouse.com*
*Phone: 1-800-839-8640*

*First published by AuthorHouse 11/26/2007*

*ISBN: 978-1-4343-4076-4 (sc)*

*Printed in the United States of America*
*Bloomington, Indiana*

*This book is printed on acid-free paper.*

To the memory of kidnapped victims who were not released unharmed.

# Contents

# Introduction

I was three weeks old when Charles A. Lindbergh, Jr. was kidnapped on March 1, 1932. Four years later, I can distinctly recall my mother and father discussing the Lindbergh case and the execution of Bruno Richard Hauptmann. I even remember which room we were in when I asked my mother "what is kidnapping?" She explained to me that it was someone "stealing a baby." Then I asked what was execution? Her answer was that the man who stole the baby was killed. Through what I consider a strange twist and turn of events, about 48 years later I was the FBI Agent who signed the final authorization to release the Lindbergh kidnapping files to the public, under the provisions of the Freedom of Information Act. I am only writing about eight kidnappings and only two of the victims were not murdered. That is not a good percentage. Actually there is no good percentage unless all victims are released unharmed.

The name of this book comes from kidnapping statutes in states that still have the death penalty.

The statutes read "...if the victim is not released unharmed, the penalty is death." In the states where there is no death penalty, kidnappers can murder their victims and they know they will not pay the ultimate price for their brutal crimes.

# Acknowledgments

My wife, Vera Owens Smith, who greatly helped with typing and reviewing the draft.

My daughter, Melody Haakenson, who edited the final draft.

Federal Bureau of Investigation, Washington, DC, that furnished documentation from its files.

The following news sources whose news articles were received from the FBI:

San Francisco Journal, San Francisco, CA

Oakland Tribune, Oakland, CA

Washington Star, Washington, DC

Los Angeles Herald Express, Los Angeles, CA

Berkeley Daily Gazette, Berkeley, CA

Times Star, Alameda, CA

San Francisco Chronicle, San Francisco, CA

San Francisco Call Bulletin, San Francisco, CA

One unidentified newspaper article, date unknown, but reporter was Gale Cook

Another unidentified newspaper article, date unknown

Front page photos of Smith as an FBI Agent and Smiths by wagon wheel

# SOMEONE KILLED THE EAGLET

When Charles A. Lindbergh made his daring solo and nonstop flight from New York City to Paris, France, he was called "The Lone Eagle." He later flew his airplane to Mexico City where he was a guest of Ambassador Dwight Morrow. There he met Mr. Morrow's daughter, Anne.

I can understand why Lindbergh fell in love with her. Without exception, the pictures which I have seen of Anne Morrow Lindbergh portray her as an absolutely beautiful woman. She could have gone to Hollywood and easily become a movie star.

After Lindbergh's marriage to Anne, their first child was a boy. They named him Charles A. Lindbergh, Jr. The child was quickly dubbed "The Eaglet." Then, millions were shocked and outraged when the 20-months-old Charles, Jr. was kidnapped on March 1, 1932. His badly decomposed body was discovered, quite accidentally, on May 12, 1932, about 4 ½ miles from the Lindbergh home at Hopewell, New Jersey. When it was announced the child had been killed a nation wept.

The last person to see the Lindbergh child alive was his nurse, Betty Gow. She put him to bed about 8:30pm, and when she went to check on him around 10:00pm his crib was empty.

Gow quickly went downstairs and asked Lindbergh whether the child was down there. She said, "Please don't play a trick on me." He replied "no, is he not in his crib?" When she said "no" Lindbergh raced quickly to the nursery, and instead of finding his child, he found a kidnap note on the windowsill, which is as follows:

1

*"Dear Sir!*
*Have 50000$ redy 25000$ in*
*20$ bills 15000$ in 10$ bills and*
*10000$ in 5$ bills After 2-4 days we will inform you were to deliver the Mony.*
*We warn you for making anyding public or for notify the Police the chld is in gute care.*
*Indication for all leters are singature and 3 hold*

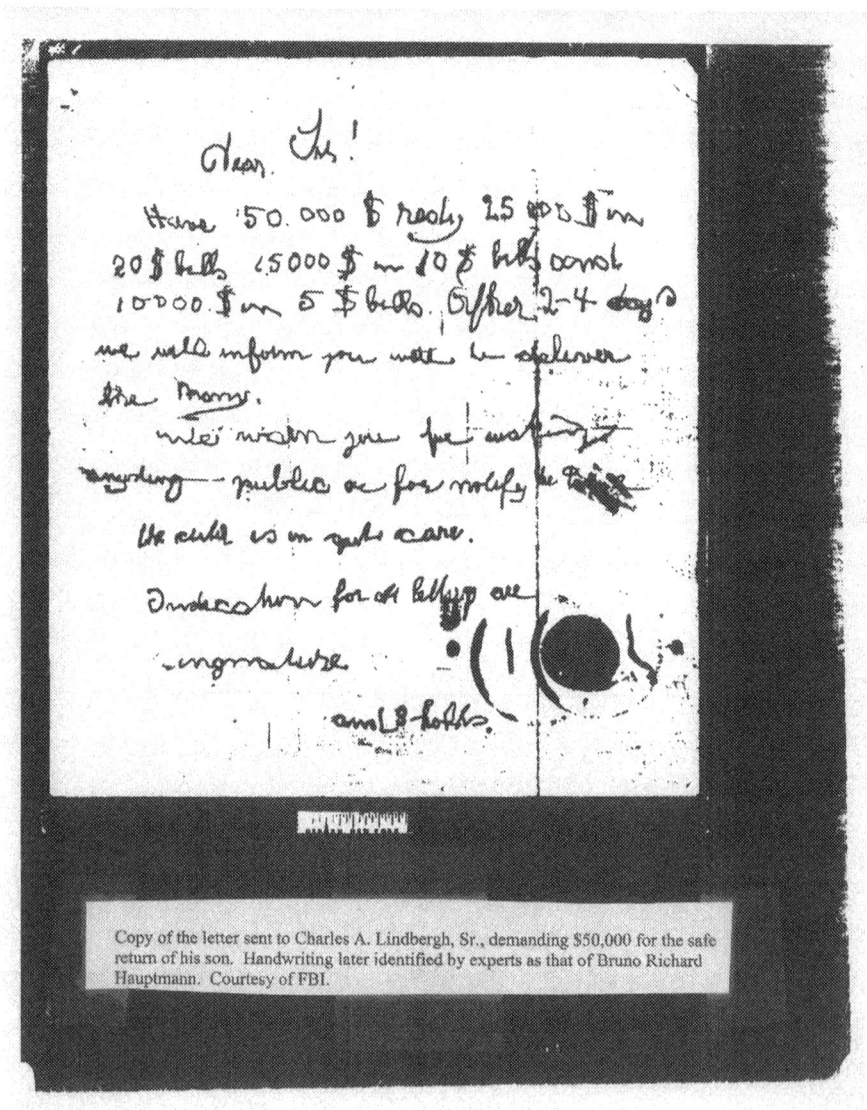

Copy of the letter sent to Charles A. Lindbergh, Sr., demanding $50,000 for the safe return of his son. Handwriting later identified by experts as that of Bruno Richard Hauptmann. Courtesy of FBI.

Below the writing were two interlocking circles with three square-like holes punched in them. Note the spelling of ready as "redy", money as "mony", anything as "anyding", child as "chld", good as "gute", letters as "leters", signature as "singnature" and hole as "hold". Later being a bad speller would come back to haunt the kidnapper. What I consider the most important is the misspelling of "signature." You will see later what I mean!

Lindbergh called the New Jersey State Police and officers were quickly on the scene. The New Jersey State Police Director was H. Norman Schwarzkopf. His son, Schwarzkopf, Jr., would later become General Schwarzkopf who, as a four star general, would command an army that drove the Iraqi army out of Kuwait.

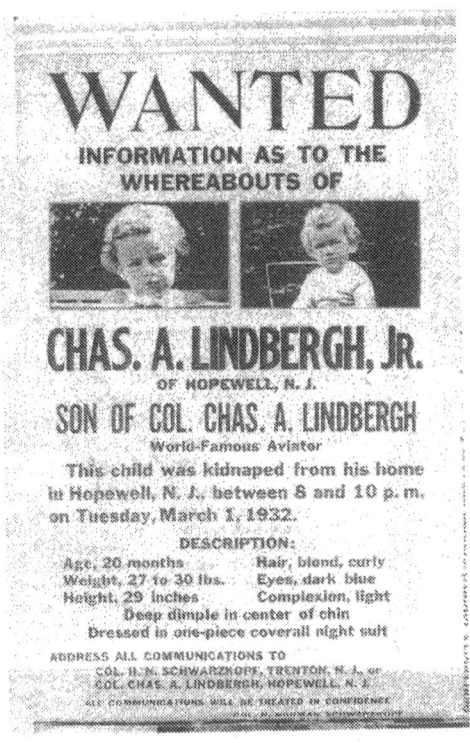

Information wanted poster issued by FBI for Charles A. Lindbergh, Jr. Courtesy of FBI.

The kidnapper made several fatal mistakes. First, he left a kidnap note with some misspellings in it. He later sent handwritten letters, and the handwriting was identical to the initial handwriting of the note left at the scene. In fact, handwriting experts determined that the handwriting in all of the notes was written by the same person. Also, he left the kidnap ladder near the house. The ladder, made in three sections, was somewhat crude, but it was ingenuously constructed. The three sections could be connected together, and extended to the upper story of the house. It was, in fact, a prototype of extension ladders today. The kidnapper would have been more wise to have patented his ladder than go for ransom. He would have made more than fifty thousand dollars. Also, the kidnapper left a ¾ inch wood chisel near the Lindbergh home, which was later determined to have come from a certain set of chisels owned by the kidnapper.

On April 2, 1932, the kidnapper accepted a ransom payoff of $50,000 (which had the serial numbers recorded), a very bad mistake. He accepted the money from Dr. John F. Condon, who was a retired educator. When the news broke that the Lindbergh child had been kidnapped Condon, without consulting Lindbergh, put an advertisement in a Bronx newspaper offering to be the go-between and added that he would give the kidnapper $1,000 of his own money, listing his address and telephone number. It came out in the investigation that Dr. Condon had never met, nor even conversed on the telephone with Lindbergh..

Another mistake made by the kidnapper was that he sent Dr. Condon a sleeping suit, and the handwriting on the package was identical to all other handwritings in this case. The sleeping suit was identified by the baby's nurse as the one she placed on him when he was put to bed. When the child's body was discovered, the sleeping suit was missing. One mistake the kidnapper did NOT make was that he left no fingerprints anywhere.

The kidnapper now began to pass the money, mainly in the area of the Bronx Borough in New York City. This was indeed a big mistake. There were several other errors made by the kidnapper, which readers will see as I continue with this case. But, I have to set out now what was probably the biggest blunder of all. On September 15, 1934, the kidnapper purchased gasoline at a service station where the attendant had, about a week before, been stuck with a counterfeit bill. So, this time the attendant recorded the license plate number of his customer. It was New York 4U-13-41. (Unlucky 13 in kidnapper's license plate?) The bill made its way through the banking procedures, and an alert clerk noticed it. The FBI and police were notified, they checked motor vehicle records, and found that 4U-13-41 was registered to Bruno Richard Hauptmann for a 1930 blue Dodge, address listed: 1279 East 222nd Street, the Bronx. This address is near where many ransom bills had been passed. Another mistake made by the kidnapper was passing money near where he lived. Officers staked out the house location all night and the next morning they observed a man driving away. He was pulled over and identified as Bruno Richard Hauptmann. In his wallet was a $20 bill that was on the ransom list.

Photograph taken by United Press International of Bruno Richard Hauptmann shortly after his arrest at 9:15 AM on September 19, 1934. When arrested by FBI Agents and officers of the New Jersey State Police and New York City Police, he had in his wallet a $20.00 bill that matched the serial number on the kidnap ransom list. Courtesy of FBI.

Division of Investigation

U. S. Department of Justice

Room 1403
370 Lexington Avenue
New York, N. Y.

THS:MT
62-3057.

September 25, 1934.

MEMORANDUM FOR FILE:

Re: BRUNO RICHARD HAUPTMANN with alias
UNKNOWN SUBJECTS
Kidnaping and Murder of Charles A. Lindbergh, Jr.

On September 25, 1934, shortly before noon, Inspector Bruckman, Agent F. E. Wright, and officers from the New Jersey State Police and New York Police, found in the nursery closet of the Hauptmann residence a piece of panel board on which had been written the following:

2974 Decatur Avenue
Sedgwick 3-7154

An obvious attempt had been made to erase the above figures. However, the address was clearly discernible to the naked eye and the telephone number could also be made out but not so clearly. The above address and telephone number were apparently written in pencil and the writing appeared to be that of Hauptmann. The importance of this lies in the fact that 2974 Decatur Avenue is the residence of Dr. Condon and has been for a good many years; also in the fact that Sedgwick 3-7154 was Dr. Condon's listed telephone up to April 12, 1932. On the date specified Dr. Condon because of the large number of cranks constantly telephoning him had the telephone in question taken out and unlisted telephone Sedgwick 3-1177 installed. It would therefore appear that if Hauptmann wrote the number Sedgwick 3-7154 on a piece of board he undoubtedly did so prior to April 12, 1932. The board on which the numbers in question were written was a piece of panel board about 6'2" long and 4" wide. It was removed from the closet and turned over to the custody of District Attorney Foley of the Bronx.

Copy of FBI memorandum showing the address and telephone number of Dr. John F. Condon, the intermediary between Lindbergh and the kidnapper. Hauptmann admitted that he wrote this information on a closet door in his home because he was interested in the case. Courtesy of FBI.

Consider the additional evidence: There was an artist's conception made of the man who had passed the ransom money, and there was a witness who reported seeing a car near the Lindbergh home before the kidnapping, with ladders stacked across the seats. When Bruno was identified as the man who had passed one of the bills to the gasoline attendant, he definitely fit the description of the man the artist drew. Also he had a 1929 Dodge described by a witness who saw a car near the Lindbergh estate before the kidnapping.

Arrested with one of the ransom-recorded bills in his wallet, he claimed he had no more such bills. However, when the FBI and police searched his house and garage they did find more ransom money. In Hauptmann's garage the investigators found $14,600, all matching the ransom list. Some bills were rolled up and stuffed into holes that had been bored in some of the lumber. Does an innocent man do this? I would say no. In the same garage they also found a chisel set with the ¾-inch chisel missing. Remember, there was a ¾-inch chisel found at the Lindbergh home. The crime scene chisel matched the chisel set in Bruno's garage.

Also, consider the following evidence developed in this case—more fatal evidence: Bruno claimed the money he had squirreled away in his garage was left with him by a man named Isidor Fisch; he and Bruno had once dabbled in fur trading. Fisch was a German, as was Bruno. In fact, Bruno was an illegal alien in the United States. He had stowed away on a ship from Germany that had docked in the harbor in New York. However, the investigators determined Fisch died a pauper in Germany.

The ransom payment was made on the night of April 2, 1932, and there is no record that Bruno ever worked another day afterwards. Yet he bought expensive items, such as a radio which cost $395, quite a bit for a carpenter during the Great Depression who was not working. Also, his wife made a trip to Germany and came back with some expensive silverware. There were also expensive vacation trips taken to California and Florida.

But what I consider one of the most convincing items of evidence is the kidnap ladder that was left at the scene. In an examination of the ladder, a man from the U. S. Forest Service was called to assist in the investigation. This man, Arthur Koehler, told the investigators that if they could find where one of the rails to a ladder section (later identified as Rail 16) came from, he could testify to this. He could identify Rail 16 having been sawed off from a particular piece of wood by matching up the grains in the two pieces. Also, most important of all, Koehler said he could testify that the four nail holes in this rail had been nailed to a particular board. He noted that the nails had been driven down in a slight slant. Also, Koehler observed that the ladder had not been planed by a machine, but by hand. He said if the hand plane could be found, he could identify it with some of the plane work in the ladder. He also declared that the chisel used to do some of the chiseling on the ladder, was a ¾ inch chisel.

Further, after a painstaking investigation some wood similar to that in the ladder was traced to a lumberyard in the Bronx near where Bruno lived and he had been a customer at this place. Rail 16 was a vital piece of evidence. When Bruno was arrested the investigators searched his house, including the attic. Of course, they were looking for money, but found none in the attic. They did notice something strange, however, and that was part of one board in the floor had been sawed off, and officers knew it had been sawed off there in the attic. How? There was an accumulation of sawdust where it had been cut. They then took Rail 16 from the ladder and placed it where the board had been sawed and where there were four nail holes. Rail 16 fit perfectly and the four nail holes in Rail 16 matched perfectly with holes in the joist. They were the old-fashioned square type nails. The nails were placed in Rail 16, lightly tapped, and they went all of the way down, flush with Rail 16. Now this is hard-core evidence!!

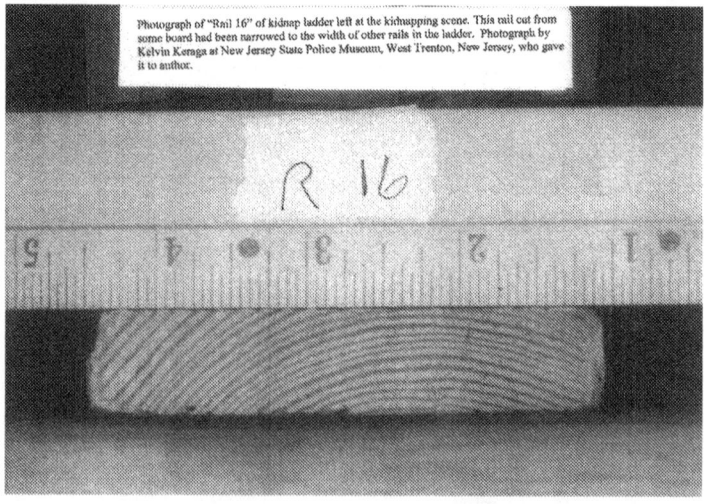

Photograph of "Rail 16" of kidnap ladder left at the kidnapping scene. This rail cut from some board had been narrowed to the width of other rails in the ladder. Photograph by Kelvin Keraga at New Jersey State Police Museum, West Trenton, New Jersey, who gave it to author.

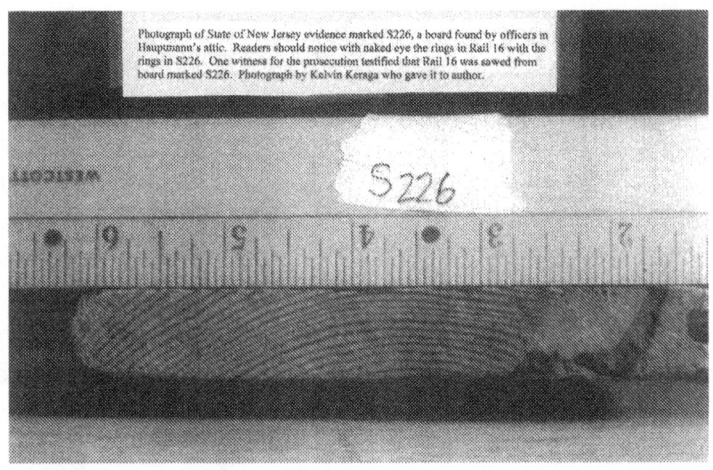

Photograph of State of New Jersey evidence marked S226, a board found by officers in Hauptmann's attic. Readers should notice with naked eye the rings in Rail 16 with the rings in S226. One witness for the prosecution testified that Rail 16 was sawed from board marked S226. Photograph by Kelvin Keraga who gave it to author.

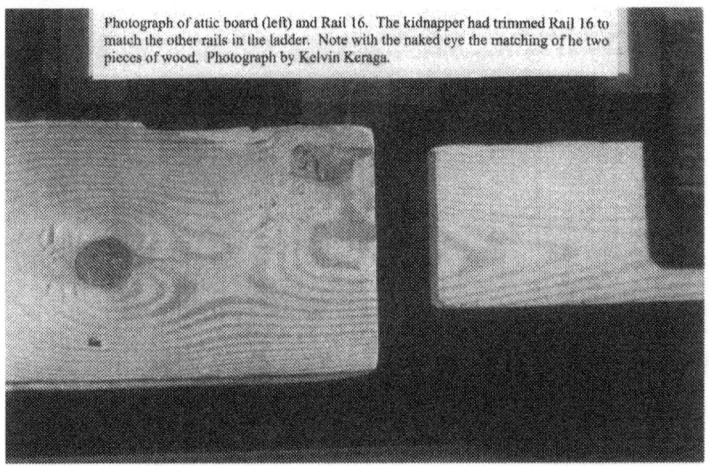

Photograph of attic board (left) and Rail 16. The kidnapper had trimmed Rail 16 to match the other rails in the ladder. Note with the naked eye the matching of he two pieces of wood. Photograph by Kelvin Keraga.

When Bruno was arrested, the investigators also found a notebook belonging to Bruno and in it was a partial sketch of a ladder similar to the ladder found at the kidnapping scene. They also discovered a dowel pin and there were dowel pins in the kidnap ladder. How did dowel pins function? I'll try to explain. There were holes bored in the rails of each section and the holes in the bottom and second section would be aligned, as well as the holes in the second and third sections. When the metal pins were inserted in the aligned holes the ladder would not come crashing down, but would hold the weight of a man.

Here is a big question: Why would Bruno go up in his attic and saw off a piece of a board? He had been a customer at a nearby lumberyard, so why didn't he simply go to the lumberyard and buy one board he needed to complete his ladder? Here is a logical answer: Some of the kind of boards in the kidnapping were of the same kind of lumber that had been shipped to the lumberyard. It was determined that Bruno had been a customer at this place. He was obviously smart enough to think this thing through. Many customers go in and buy several boards at a time, and it is believed Bruno had made the same kind of purchase. The lumberyard did not keep records of purchases by name, and customers going in and out would not be remembered in any detail. But suppose one customer bought several pieces and then came back a little later and bought only one board? That was something a clerk could have remembered months later. This was another fatal mistake Bruno made. If he had been smart enough, he would have gone back and purchased only one board, and taken the chance that the clerk would not have remembered. But Bruno did not go back. He went up into his attic and sawed off the one board he needed to complete his "extension ladder". This fatal mistake helped send him to the electric chair.

Then there was Cecile Barr who worked selling tickets at a movie theatre. She positively identified Bruno as a patron who passed one of the ransom bills. How could she possibly identify Bruno as buying a ticket several months before? Here is how. She was in the process of closing out for the evening, viz., counting money and tickets sold, etc. Then, through her peripheral vision she saw someone throw down in front of her a bill that was folded three times, creating impressions of eight squares. When she looked up she saw a man standing at her window. She asked which ticket he wanted. The theatre had areas of seating which were priced differently. The patron only spoke two words, "forty-two"--meaning a 42 cents seat. Later, she was a witness who could not be crossed up by the defense. She identified Bruno in court as the man who passed her a bill that was on the ransom list, having thrown it down in front of her, folded three times.

Bruno should not have done something so memorable as throwing a bill down in front of Barr that was folded three times, and at a time when she was closing out her daily receipts. This was a big mistake.

After Bruno's arrest not one single ransom note was passed anywhere.

There were handwriting experts who testified that known handwriting of Bruno's was identical to the handwriting on the kidnap letters. When he was first in custody he gave handwriting specimens to the arresting officers. But they did not stop there, the investigators obtained Bruno's handwriting from his applications for car insurance, driver's license and from other documents. Further, in some of the handwriting specimens that Bruno gave there were misspellings of the same words as in the kidnap notes. All of these specimens were compared with the kidnap letters, and it was determined by highly qualified handwriting experts that Bruno wrote all of the notes.

Of course, there was also a handwriting examiner who was hired by the defense team. He testified that Bruno did not write the kidnap letters. Obviously, no handwriting "expert" for the defense would be hired if he did not say Bruno did not write the notes. Apparently the jury did not put any credence in his testimony. There were 21 who said yes Bruno did write the kidnap letters and only one who said he did not. There was compelling and overwhelming evidence that Bruno wrote the kidnap notes.

There is something else Bruno wrote that became evidence. When the officers searched his house one noticed on a wood facing of a closet door this writing: "2974 Decatur Avenue Sedwick 3-7154." Whose address was this and whose telephone number? It appeared that someone had attempted to erase this. Bruno admitted that he had written it. It was the address and telephone number of Dr. John F. Condon who was the intermediary who identified in court that Bruno was the man he met in the cemetery and to whom he paid $50,000 in ransom money. Why did he write this, Bruno was asked? He was interested in the case, he claimed. He most assuredly was interested in it because he collected $50,000 in ransom money!

Then there was a witness for the defense, Bruno Richard Hauptmann. When examined by defense attorneys he denied all elements of the kidnapping/murder. I learned years ago there is a danger for any defendant to testify for himself. Bruno's lawyer further asked him whether when he was in police custody if they told him to spell and write the word signature as "singnature". He replied that they did. Now, the prosecutor had his turn to cross-examine Bruno. David T. Wilentz, the New Jersey Attorney General and main attorney for the prosecution, showed no mercy and no pity for Bruno. He turned him every which way but loose and bounced him from one end of the courtroom to the other. There are those who have said that Bruno was the "...best possible witness for the prosecution." I am inclined to agree, and for someone like Wilentz who had never before prosecuted a capital case, he was masterful. During the cross examination Wilentz questioned Bruno about what he had testified—that he was instructed to write signature as "singnature". At this point Wilentz dropped a bombshell on Bruno and his defense lawyers. He picked up the handwriting specimens given by Bruno to the police, walked over to the jury, and laid them in front of them. He told the jury to go through these specimens and nowhere would they find Bruno's handwriting of the word "signature." He explained that when the police were obtaining handwriting specimens from Bruno, they purposely did not ask him to write the word "signature." This sent Bruno and his attorney team picking up the pieces and staggering away.

How much more evidence would a prosecutor need? None. It is interesting, however, to note the evidence that Wiltenz did NOT use. I'll get into that shortly. Wiltenz had so much evidence he obviously did not believe he needed more. In fact, I guess he didn't. However, as an FBI Agent I never believed in, nor ever desired, a U. S. Attorney to limit the number of witnesses--or any other evidence . If there were five witnesses who identified John Doe as the man who robbed the bank, I wanted all five to testify.

When I was in the FBI, assigned in Oklahoma, I interviewed a former bank manager who had been caught with his hand in the till. When he was confronted with the evidence the FBI had, he said he was "...as guilty as a sheep killing dog." So was Bruno.

Another big mistake Bruno made was choosing to kidnap a child of an around the world hero. From the United States to South America, to Europe, to China, people were calling for Bruno's hide. When Bruno was arrested with a $20 ransom bill in his wallet, quite frankly he was on his way to the electric chair. He could have started counting off the days and hours until his execution.

The "Bruno was innocent" folks have asked, and quite appropriately: "how did the kidnapper know that the Lindbergh family was not going back that Tuesday (March 1, 1932) to the Morrow home in Englewood,

New Jersey, as they usually did?" Lindbergh commuted to and from downtown New York City where he was a consultant to two large airlines. Then the family would go back to Hopewell on the weekends and back to the Morrow home on Tuesday morning. But that Tuesday the baby was sick and they stayed overnight. Also, how would the kidnapper know where the nursery room was in order to place the ladder under that window and steal the baby? I'll speculate later.

Some unused evidence was this: When investigators searched Bruno's garage, they found a keg of nails, not unusual for a carpenter to have. However, this keg of nails helped send Bruno to his death. When Arthur Koehler was called in to help in the investigation, he took the ladder apart, board-by-board. There were 44 nails in the ladder which were identified by a small marking as having been made by the Pittsburgh Steel Company. There were also nails with the same markings used when Bruno's garage was built. Bruno built it. Information was developed that the Pittsburgh Steel Company had manufactured and shipped to customers 16 kegs of nails, one hundred pounds each, in a particular "batch". One keg showed up in Bruno's garage.

Let's consider this. What are the odds that the nails in Bruno's garage did NOT come from that keg of nails the investigators found in his garage? The odds are so high that I cannot calculate them. Would not an ordinary, reasonable, prudent person conclude that they came from the keg investigators found? Of course, they came from that keg in Bruno's garage! Now remember there is strong evidence that Rail 16 came from Bruno's attic. Again, what are the odds that the 44 nails in the ladder also came from Bruno's keg of nails. Something to think about, is it not? If the nail evidence had been introduced by the prosecution, it would have served to drive yet another nail in Bruno's coffin. (Pardon the pun.)

Remember, one of the rails in the ladder split and there are those who suggest that the additional weight of the baby is what caused the board to split. But let's not stop with speculation but consider this. I have an FBI memorandum dated September 24, 1934, and it sets out information that shortly after the kidnapping Bruno visited Dr. Otto Meyer, 200 W. 54th Street, New York City, with a leg injury. He told Dr. Meyer his injury was a result of a fall from a ladder while working at his trade as a carpenter.

The Hauptmann supporters have used the "Violet Sharpe matter" as evidence that points to Bruno's innocence. Sharpe was one of about 29 servants who worked in the Morrow household. It was Sharpe who answered the telephone on the morning of March 1, 1932, when Mrs. Lindbergh called and told Sharpe to have Betty Gow come to Hopewell to help care for the baby who had a cold and cough. With this call, soon everyone in the Morrow household knew the Lindberghs and the child were staying overnight on that particular Tuesday.

Sharpe had immigrated from Scotland to work as a servant. She was liked by all in the Morrow household, especially a butler named Septimus Banks. Some thought Banks and Sharpe would soon marry. After the kidnapping, the police interviewed everyone in the Morrow household. When they got around to Sharpe she was evasive in answering their questions. They asked for her activities on the evening of the kidnapping and she said she had gone to a movie with some friends. Who were the friends? She could not remember. Then, which movie did she see? She could not remember that either. After a grilling interview the police officers said they would be back for more questioning. But before the time of this impending appointment Violet Sharpe drank a toxic solution of silver polish and dropped dead.

Why would Sharpe kill herself if she were totally innocent? Good question. For those who believe someone was involved with the kidnapper, Sharpe was a good person to consider. However, after seeing the newspaper headlines about the police interrogation of Sharpe, the three friends she had been with that evening came forward and told the police they had been with her that evening. They were Ernest Miller, Elmer Johnson and Elmer's date, Katherine Minners.

Sharpe had been in the hospital having her tonsils out, and left even though her doctor advised that she should stay. There are those who contend that Sharpe was involved sexually with more than one man. I have discovered a matter which some researchers have overlooked. In a 450-page FBI summary report setting out an investigation from March 1, 1932, until February 1, 1934, there is something interesting. The FBI said, "According to an informant presently employed at the Englewood residence of the Morrow family, Violet Sharpe spent a great deal of her time in the company of Septimus Banks, the Morrow butler; they appeared to be in love with each other and several months prior to the kidnapping Violet Sharpe underwent an abortion operation necessitated by her intimacy with Banks."

Now here is the big question. Who was the "informant" in the Morrow household? Based on my experiences as an FBI agent, this "informant" would not have been an informant in the usual sense. The FBI opens informant cases on people who are sometimes contacted for criminal information, or furnish national security information. Certainly there was no criminal nor national security activity going on in the Morrow household. But in this instance the FBI was simply refraining from putting someone's name in a report, probably based on the fact that the person had requested confidentiality. I believe the source was Septimus Banks. Who else would have known Violet was pregnant? It is possible that Violet, not wanting all of this to be discovered, chose suicide.

Sharpe admitted that she once dated a man named McKelvie who worked for a New York City newspaper. It was reported that when the Lindbergh child was born (in the Morrow mansion) Sharpe leaked the information to McKelvie that the baby was a boy. This enabled McKelvie's newspaper to get a "scoop" about four hours ahead of other newspapers.

Also, I have a friend who is a retired school counselor, Keith Roylance. He has a graduate degree in psychology and has briefly studied this kidnapping case. He told me that he "would not doubt" that Violet Share was duped into assisting in the kidnapping with a promise that the baby would not be harmed, but when she learned the baby was killed, she took her own life.

What do I think? I do not believe that she knowingly and willingly was involved in the case. I do believe it is possible that Sharpe, after talking to Mrs. Lindbergh and being told they were staying over that night at Hopewell, could have answered the telephone another time on March 1, 1932. Who knows? Maybe that was her duty. A call could have gone like this: " I'd like to speak to Mr. Lindbergh."

"He is not here."

"What time will he be back?"

"He won't be back today, the baby is sick and they are staying overnight again at Hopewell." Of course, this is pure speculation, but I'm trying to explain Violet Sharpe. She just simply will not go away.

The FBI and police have resolved a lot of matters where people would confess to the kidnapping of the Lindbergh child. Invariably, these people did not fit the description given by witnesses who received some of the ransom notes, did not know what the baby was wearing, did not know the layout of the Lindbergh home, did not speak with a German accent, and among other things, were not caught spending and being in possession of the ransom money. Further, when Dr. Condon met that night in a graveyard in the Bronx, he showed the kidnapper two larger-than-normal safety pins. Dr. Condon asked whether he recognized the pins and he declared that "yes, they were used to pin down the child's covers."

Shortly after Bruno became a suspect, an FBI Special Agent Accountant named J. A. Genau conducted an extensive investigation into Bruno's financial activities. He submitted his report on October 8, 1934, which consisted of 63 pages. Keep in mind that when the police and FBI searched Bruno's garage and house they found approximately $14,600, all of which was Lindbergh kidnap ransom money. Some of the money was rolled up and stuffed in holes that had been bored in pieces of wood. Now is this something an innocent man would do? I would think not.

Agent Genau set out on page 50 of his report where actual CASH deposits had been made to six accounts belonging to Bruno Richard Hauptmann and his wife, Anna Schoeffler. These cash deposits, beginning after April 2, 1932, came to a total of $26,016. "Source unknown." The last transaction in these six accounts, a $500 deposit, occurred on September 17,1934. Bruno was arrested on September 19, 1934. But Agent Genau's accounting evidence was never used. He was not called as a witness.

There have been books written, speeches made, private investigators hired, and evidence re-examined by those who contend Hauptmann was innocent. But the real problems for these Bruno defenders do not even begin until they are asked to give an explanation of the money. Bruno's own explanation about the money, his lying about it, and his shifting and squirming are sources of embarrassment to the Bruno defenders.

62-3057

The following schedules reflect the actual cash deposited and withdrawals made by Richard Hauptmann and wife through brokerage houses and banks since April 2, 1932:

## CASH DEPOSITS

| DATE 1932 | CENTRAL SAVINGS BANK | CARLETON AND MOTT | MT. VERNON TRUST COMPANY | STEINER, ROUSE & CO. R. HAUPTMANN | STEINER, ROUSE & CO. ANNA SCHOEFFLER | THE MANHAT SAVINGS INSTITUTI |
|---|---|---|---|---|---|---|
| Apr. 5 | 87.00 | | | | | |
| 8 | 27.00 | | | | | |
| 8 | | 600.00 | | | | |
| 11 | | 22.75 | | | | |
| 18 | 160.00 | | | | | |
| 25 | 41.00 | | | | | |
| May 4 | 55.00 | | | | | |
| 16 | 200.00 | | | | | |
| 23 | 110.00 | | | | | |
| June 1 | 125.00 | | | | | |
| 1 | | | 52.00 | | | |
| 6 | 44.00 | | | | | |
| 16 | | | 105.00 | | | |
| 23 | | | 20.00 | | | |
| 30 | 50.00 | | | | | |
| July 5 | | | 75.00 | | | |
| 6 | | | 12.00 | | | |
| 15 | 80.00 | | | | | |
| 25 | 202.00 | | | | | |
| Aug. 11 | | | 84.00 | | | |
| 19 | 84.00 | | | | | |
| 20 | 43.00 | | | | | |
| 29 | 90.00 | | | | | |
| 31 | | | 40.00 | | | |
| Sept. 14 | | | 259.75 | | | |
| 15 | | | | 170.00 | | |
| 19 | | | | 582.50 | | |
| 19 | 250.00 | | | | | |
| 22 | | | 200.00 | | | |
| 26 | 150.00 | | | | | |
| Oct. 26 | 147.00 | | | | | |
| 27 | | | | | 860.00 | |
| 31 | 140.00 | | | | | |
| 27 | | | 132.00 | | | |
| Nov. 28 | | | 138.00 | | | |

- 50 -

Pages 50 and 51 of FBI Accounting report showing deposits by Hauptmann from April 5, 1932, (three days after ransom payment) through September 17, 1934. Hauptmann's house was placed under surveillance by the FBI and police on September 18, 1934, and he was arrested the following morning with one of the ransom bills in his wallet. All of this time Hauptmann was unemployed.

17

62-3057

| DATE 1933 | CENTRAL SAVINGS BANK | CARLETON AND MOTT | MT. VERNON TRUST COMPANY | STEINER, ROUSE & CO. R. HAUPTMANN | STEINER, ROUSE & CO. ANNA SCHOEFFLER | THE MANHATTAN SAVINGS INSTITUTION |
|---|---|---|---|---|---|---|
| Jan. 10 | $1,287.50 | $ | $ | $ | $ | $ |
| 10 | | | 139.00 | | | |
| 16 | | | 186.00 | | | |
| Feb. 15 | | | 230.00 | | | |
| 17 | 60.00 | | | | | |
| 27 | | | | 700.00 | | |
| Mar. 1 | | | | 850.00 | | |
| 3 | | | 55.00 | | | |
| 13 | 1,250.00 | | | | | |
| Apr. 3 | 400.00 | | | | | |
| 28 | | | | | 2,500.00 | |
| May 3 | | | | | 2,575.00 | |
| June 5 | | | | | 2,225.00 | |
| July 20 | 2,000.00 | | | | | |
| 24 | | | | | 4,500.00 | |
| Aug. 10 | | | | | 7.50 | |
| 1934 Feb. 26 | | | | | 1,350.00 | |
| Aug. 20 | | | | | | 130.00 |
| Sept. 1 | | | | | | 40.00 |
| 11 | | | | | | 40.00 |
| 17 | | | | | | 50.00 |
| | $7,065.50 | $ 622.75 | $1,727.75 | $3,162.50 | $13,157.50 | $260.00 |

RECAPITULATION

| | |
|---|---|
| Central Savings Bank | 7,065.50 |
| Carleton & Mott | 622.75 |
| Mt. Vernon Trust Co. | 1,727.75 |
| Steiner, Rouse & Co. (R. Hauptmann a/c) | 3,162.50 |
| Steiner, Rouse & Co. (Anna Schoeffler a/c) | 13,157.50 |
| The Manhattan Savings Institution | 260.00 |
| Total | $25,016.00 |

- 51 -

It has been said and written by the supporters of Hauptmann that there were no fingerprints in the case that were identical to Hauptmann's fingerprints. Let's consider this. There was a detailed plan to kidnap the Lindbergh child, build the extension ladder, write the notes, and meet at night in a graveyard with the intermediary. Would the kidnapper, whoever he was, be so careless as to leave his fingerprints? No, he would not.

The supporters of Bruno contend he did not get a fair trial. Under today's standards he certainly did not; but guilty he was. There is something else to consider: When Bruno was arrested the investigators found, among other items, a pair of binoculars. That Tuesday evening or even before, the kidnapper could have easily observed someone with the baby (his crib was next to a window) in the nursery. The house was new and there were things for this new house that had not been completed, such as curtains and window shades. I have seen a photograph of the baby's room pointing directly to the window entered by the kidnapper, and there were no curtains or shades.

Let's go back. How did the kidnapper know the Lindberghs were staying over on March 1, 1932? Maybe it was just good luck for the kidnapper that the baby was there that fateful evening. This could have been. Further, on Tuesday, March 1, 1932, there were news items in New York newspapers that Lindbergh was making a presentation at Columbia University in New York City that evening. The kidnapper could have read the newspapers and concluded that the man of the house was going to be late getting home. As it turned out Lindbergh, with his busy schedule, forgot about this appointment and returned home around 8:30pm.

Bruno told the investigators that he had no previous criminal record. It was a big mistake to lie about this. The FBI contacted the German Nazi Government to determine if he did, in fact, have a criminal past. He did. The Identification Service, Berlin, Germany, furnished information as follows:

*"As Bruno Hauptmann 6/3/1919, joint great robbery, 2 years, 1 week prison – 4 years loss of civic rights." "Of joint highway robbery 2 years, 6 months prison – 2 years loss of civic rights." Bruno was a native of Saxony, Germany.*

19

Bruno was born November 26, 1889, was convicted for the kidnapping and murder of the Lindbergh child, and was sentenced to death, and executed on April 3, 1936. He never confessed. While he was in police custody there were indications that he had been beaten. But this was irrelevant--they did not beat any type of an admission out of him.

Shortly after the execution, one of Bruno's lawyers made a public statement that the execution of Bruno was the greatest tragedy in the history of New Jersey. Not so! If I had to make a list of tragedies in New Jersey, I would list near, or at the top, the kidnapping and murder of a 20-month-old baby. I would put Bruno at the bottom of the list, if I even listed him at all.

When the jury first reached the jury room for deliberations, they immediately took a vote and found Bruno guilty of murder in the first degree. Then they voted whether or not to recommend mercy. It was 11 to one NOT to recommend mercy. One holdout for mercy, one of four women, after 11 hours gave in. This condemned Bruno to the electric chair.

# "DON'T SHOOT G-MEN, DON'T SHOOT G-MEN!"

As an FBI agent I spent several years assigned in Elizabethtown, Kentucky. There I became friends with an attorney who never called me Don, but always addressed me as "G-Man." Of course, it was a nickname that I relished. But, have you ever wondered how FBI Agents got the nickname "G-Men"? Here is how.

At 11:15 pm on July 22, 1933, Charles F. Urschel (a very wealthy Oklahoma oil man) and his wife were visiting with Walter R. Jarrett and his wife. They were sitting on a screened porch, obviously because of the blistering Oklahoma heat. Two men, one armed with a machine gun and the other with a pistol, burst onto the screened porch and demanded to know which man was Mr. Urschel. Apparently there was a moment's hesitation, and then one of the gunmen said that they would take both men. They put Urschel and Jarrett in the back of their car and drove rapidly away.

There had been a public announcement by the U. S. Attorney General, that in such an incident as this, people were to call the Director of the Federal Bureau of Investigation, J. Edgar Hoover. Although the two women had been warned not to call for help, Mrs. Urschel immediately telephoned Hoover.

At 1:00am on July 23rd, Jarrett made his way back to the Urschel home. After the kidnappers determined which man was Urschel, they released Jarrett only after taking the fifty dollars he had in his wallet. They warned Jarrett not to give anyone the directions the kidnappers had taken. After several days passed without any word about Urschel,

J. G. Catlett (a wealthy oilman in Tulsa and a close friend to Urschel) received a package. It contained a letter written by Urschel requesting Catlett to act as intermediary. The package also contained a letter to Mrs.Urschel and a typewritten note to Catlett. The kidnappers demanded that Catlett immediately proceed to Oklahoma City. He was instructed not to communicate in any manner with the Urschel family. There was also a letter for a Mr. E. E. Kirkpatrick of Oklahoma City, stating that immediately upon receipt of the letter, he was to obtain $200,000 in $20 bills. Kirkpatrick was instructed to then place an ad in the *Daily Oklahoman* newspaper that said:

*"FOR SALE—160 Acres Land, five room house, deep well. Also Cows, Tools, Tractor, Corn, and Hay. $3,750 for quick sale, TERMS..Box #."*

The ad was to run for a week. It was promptly placed.

On July 28th an Oklahoma City newspaper received a letter postmarked Joplin, Missouri, addressed to Kirkpatrick. In part it said to take $200,000 in a light--colored bag and take a train from Oklahoma City to Kansas City, Missouri. Kirkpatrick was to ride on the observation platform and look for someone between Oklahoma City and Kansas City. The kidnappers gave further instructions: Kirkpatrick was to take train #28 (The Sooner) departing from Oklahoma City at 10:10pm via the M. K. & T. Lines for Kansas City. He may observe someone between the two cities, and somewhere he would observe a fire on the right side of the track. The first fire was to alert him that there will be a second fire. He was to be prepared to throw the moneybag on the track immediately after passing the second fire. He was to leave on Saturday, July 29th. A warning was given threatening the life of Urschel if the kidnappers were double-crossed "DOUBLE XX."

Unknown to the kidnappers, Catlett rode just inside the observation car and Kirkpatrick sat on the observation platform. However, there were no fire signals along the way. When they got to Kansas City, Catlett and Kirkpatrick registered at the Muehleback Hotel. Kirkpatrick registered under the name of E. E. Kincaid. He waited in his room. Then he received a telegram advising, "Owing to unavoidable incident unable to keep appointment. Will phone you about six. C. H. Moore." At 5:30pm, July 30, Kirkpatrick received a telephone call. The caller claimed he was Moore and asked if Kirkpatrick had received the telegram. Kirkpatrick said he had. He was told to take a cab to the LaSalle Hotel and walk west a block or two. Kirkpatrick requested to have a friend with him. Of course this was denied.

Kirkpatrick followed instructions, arriving at the LaSalle Hotel at about 6:00pm. He had walked less than a half of a block when a man approached him saying, "Mr. Kincaid, I will take the bag." The man taking the bag of money told Kirkpatrick that Urschel would be released later. Kirkpatrick went back to Oklahoma City and Catlett returned to Tulsa.

Urschel was released and returned home at 11:30pm, July 31st. As soon as he recovered from his ordeal he was interviewed by FBI agents. His statement about the kidnapping was substantially the same as Jarrett's. The following is a synopsis of the information he furnished: After Jarrett's release, Urschel was blindfolded, cotton was placed in his ears and tape over his mouth. He was placed in the trunk of the car. After about an hour, the car passed some oil wells where Urschel could hear the pumping noise. When the kidnappers needed gasoline, one took the victim out in a brush area while the other went and got gasoline. He was gone about 15 minutes. About an hour later, a stop was made to open a gate; after about three minutes another stop was made to open a gate. Then, within a minute, the car was driven into what Urschel believed was a garage. In this building, they transferred the license plate to a larger car, possibly a Cadillac or Buick. Urschel was transferred to this new vehicle. They drove for two or three hours and made another stop for fuel. He heard the woman station attendant comment to one of the kidnappers that the "crops around are burned up, although they may make some broom corn."

At about 9:00 or 10:00am it rained and the road was slippery. On one occasion one of the men got out and pushed the car. At the next stop they went directly to what Urschel believed was a garage. He asked one of the men what time it was, and he replied 2:30pm. They remained in this building until dark and then proceeded. When they later reached their destination, Urschel was led into a house and into a room where there were two beds. He occupied one that was apparently an iron cot, and one of the kidnappers slept on the other. Here he heard barnyard animals.

One of two ranch houses near Paradise, Texas in which wealthy
Oklahoma oilman Charles F. Urschel was held captive following
his kidnapping. He was later released unharmed. Courtesy of FBI.

Shortly after entering the house he heard voices of a man and woman. Urschel stayed in the house until the next day, July 24th, when the two men took him in a car to another house reached in about 15 minutes driving time. At this house he ate at a small table. Here he heard the voices of a man and woman, but not the same voices he had earlier heard. Shortly, the man and woman left. On the first night at the second house he was handcuffed on one wrist with the other handcuff fastened to a chair. The kidnappers asked him if he knew a man in Tulsa, Oklahoma, who could be trusted. He named John G. Catlett and was compelled to write a letter to him. At one time Urschel was guarded by an old man and a young man. One of the men told him they had been stealing for 25 years. They said Bonnie and Clyde (Bonnie Parker and Clyde Barrow) were just a couple of cheap, filling-station robbers and car thieves. The man freely discussed a number of bank robberies, advising that he and his friend had been invited to participate in a bank robbery in Clinton, Oklahoma. (As an FBI agent I once arrested a fugitive in Clinton.) They declined because of an unfavorable "get-away" plan. Now with the blindfold removed, Urschel observed chickens, cows and hogs around the place, and he was informed by one of the men that there were four cows there. Urschel was given water from an old tin cup. The water was drawn from a well by a rope and bucket on a pulley. Also, he heard an airplane around 9:45am and 5:45pm each day; however, on Sunday, July 30, it rained very hard and the morning airplane did not come over.

On July 31st, at about 2:00pm one of the men returned and told him he was going to be released. He said that they had to leave at a certain time, and that another car was going to be a pilot car. He was then driven to a point near Norman, Oklahoma, where he was given $10 and released.

No efforts were made by the FBI until after the release of Urschel. After his release the FBI conducted an extensive investigation throughout the country. As an FBI agent we often solved tough cases by coming into some good luck. And good luck happened in this case. On July 24, 1933, a mere two days into the kidnapping, the FBI received information at Fort Worth, Texas, that the kidnappers were George "Machine Gun" Kelly and his wife, Kathryn.

But who gave the FBI this information?  Do I know for sure?  No I don't, but here is what I'd look for. The FBI files tell us the information came from Fort Worth, Texas.  Also let me point out here that in this kidnapping case there were 21 people convicted for felony violations, with sentences ranging from life in prison, down to probation and not even going to prison.  So how many of these people who were convicted regarding this matter lived in Fort Worth?  Only one that I can find. Her name was Louise Magness.

At the time the victim was being held at Paradise, Texas, Kathryn Kelly was residing with Magness.  Shortly after the ransom was paid, Magness flew to Des Moines, Iowa, where she joined George and Kathryn Kelly.  Magness then drove with the Kellys from Iowa to Brownwood, Texas.  There, posing as the sister of Kathryn, she purchased for the Kellys a 1928 Chevrolet sedan.  Magness was later convicted for harboring the Kellys and was sentenced to one year and one day.  She was sent to the federal prison for women at Alderson, West Virginia.

I am not too sure that I would go out on a limb and say that Magness was the one who gave the information to the FBI in Fort Worth that the kidnappers were George and Kathryn Kelly.  So let's discuss at least one other possibility.

What community is near Forth Worth?  Paradise, Texas is--just a few miles northwest of Fort Worth.  Kathryn Kelly's step-brother, Armon Shannon, lived a short distance from his father and stepmother, Mr. and Mrs. Shannon.  Armon was one of the 21 people who were later convicted regarding this kidnapping. All of them received jail time, except Armon.  His sentence was 10 years probation.  He never had to hear that steel door slamming and opening everyday.  Did Armon escape confinement because he was the source in Fort Worth who told the FBI who the kidnappers were?  Did the court take this into consideration when handing out his sentence?  I wish I knew.

George got this nickname reportedly because he could knock walnuts off of a fence with a submachine gun at 25 yards, without hitting the fence.  I doubt this is true for this reason: When I became an FBI agent I went through firearms training at the FBI Academy, Quantico, Virginia.  Among other weapons, we fired the Thompson submachine gun, called a "Tommy Gun", but only for the experience.

When the gun was fired, the recoil would kick it up slightly. The shooter had to work to keep bringing it down a bit. A Tommy Gun is not a weapon for firing at a small bull's eye target and trying to fire each round into the bull's eye. With the submachine gun all one had to do was spray a burst of rounds and one probably would hit or come close to hitting a target. By the time I became a Special Agent, the submachine guns were replaced in the field by the 12-gauge shotgun, loaded with double-ought buck shells.

When George married Kathryn, she encouraged him to begin a life of crime. He began running illegal alcohol and robbing banks prior to the Urschel kidnapping. He had previously served a prison sentence in New Mexico.

Here is how the FBI learned where Urschel was in Texas. They began with a review of all airline schedules within a 600-mile radius of Oklahoma City. They learned that American Airlines had two flights daily, and the flights would be in the vicinity of Paradise, Texas, at about 9:40am and about 5:40pm. Then one day one of the flights took an extreme northerly course to avoid a rainstorm. The FBI learned that Kathryn's mother and stepfather, Mr. and Mrs. R. G. Shannon, lived near Paradise, Texas. A close look at the Shannon residence was made by an undercover FBI Agent and he noted that the surroundings matched the description furnished by Urschel. It was also determined that R. G. Shannon's son, Armon Shannon, lived on a ranch about a mile-and-a-half from his father. At Armon's residence it was discovered there was a well, a water bucket, a tin cup, and it had the general surroundings described by Urschel. Further investigation revealed that George and Kathryn had been in the area during the time in question. Urschel was taken to the home of the Shannons and immediately identified the house in which he was held. He also identified Armon's house in which he was held until his release. He identified other things: the tin cup, the mineral taste of the water, and the barnyard animals around the area. Mr. and Mrs. Shannon were questioned thoroughly and readily admitted that Urschel had been held in their house. The Shannons informed the FBI that the kidnappers were George and Albert L. Bates. Bates had a lengthy criminal record and was taken into custody at Denver, Colorado on August 12, 1933, on a local charge. At the time of his arrest he had on him $660 listed as part of the ransom money, and he too was in possession of a machine gun.

Now the hunt was on for George and Kathryn Kelly. The FBI received information that they were living at the home of a man named J. C. Tichenor in Memphis, Tennessee. In the early morning hours of September 26, 1933, the FBI and Memphis police officers conducted a raid on the home of Tichenor. Caught without a weapon in his hands, Kelly screamed, "Don't shoot G-men! Don't shoot G-Men!" There you have it; this is how FBI agents got the name of "G- men."

George R. Kelly. He had served a sentence in the New Mexico State Prison, and was known to be enjoying many luxuries, including high-powered automobiles and expensive jewelry, without any visible means of support.

George "Machine Gun" Kelly

Kelly was born in Tennessee in 1897, and spent his early years in modest surroundings. He attended public schools before becoming a salesman and, later, a bootlegger. He married Kathryn Thorne in 1927. She encouraged Kelly to become deeply involved in a life of crime, bought him a machine gun, and gave him the nickname, "Machine Gun". He concentrated on running illegal alcohol and also robbery.

On October 12, 1933, George and Kathryn were convicted and George was sentenced to life imprisonment and Kathryn to 20 years. Tichenor was convicted for harboring the Kellys and was sentenced to two years and six months in prison. Among many others who were convicted and went to prison regarding the kidnapping and harboring the Kellys were Kathryn's mother and stepfather, Mr. and Mrs. R. G. Shannon. They were sentenced to life in prison. Armon Shannon got off easy with his sentence of only 10 years probation.

But here is the good part:  One person who was charged with receiving ransom money was a Denver attorney named Ben Laska, who ended up in Leavenworth. And, this is not all. There was another Denver attorney named Mollie O. Bert who was indicted for perjury during the trial of Laska.  After a plea of not guilty, she was released on $5,000 bond.  She later withdrew her not guilty plea and entered a plea of "nolle contendere." This is a Latin phrase which means the charges are not contested and it has the same effect as a guilty plea.  Bert was sentenced to one year and one day, but the sentence was suspended pending good behavior for one year.  Now this is what I consider a good case ending, when the lawyers for people in a criminal case are also convicted.

"Machine Gun" Kelly died of a heart attack in the Federal Prison at Leavenworth, Kansas. Kathryn Kelly, according to FBI documents, was last known to be in Oklahoma.  Indeed she was.  As a new FBI Agent I was assigned in Oklahoma City.  During the time I was there, Kathryn Kelly, after her parole, was working in the courthouse.  I had thought about going to the office in which she was working, introducing myself, shaking hands with her, and asking for an autograph.  However, I never did for this reason: Had FBI Director J. Edgar Hoover learned about this I could, or might have been, suspended for two or three weeks for conduct unbecoming an FBI Agent.  I was married and had a small family and I could not afford to be docked two or three weeks in pay.

# A "CLASS ACT" BY FBI AGENTS

On May 24, 1935, at Tacoma, Washington, George Weyerhaeuser, the nine-years-old son of J. P. Weyerhaeuser, disappeared on his way home from school. That evening a special delivery letter addressed "To whom it may concern" demanding a $200,000 ransom was demanded in twenty, ten and five dollar bills. George's signature was on the back of the envelope. The kidnappers instructed that an ad be placed under the "Personal" column in a Seattle newspaper. The ad was to be signed "Percy Minnie" and was to run in the newspaper on May 27 and May 29, 1935. On May 29, 1935, the boy's father received a letter from the kidnappers instructing him to register as "James Paul Jones" at the Ambassador Hotel in Seattle. That night a taxicab driver delivered another letter to him, giving instructions to drive to a designated place where he would find two sticks driven into the ground with a piece of white cloth attached. There he found another message directing him to another signal. However, he found no message there. Weyerhaeuser waited two hours, and then returned to his hotel.

On May 30, 1935, the boy's father received a telephone call accusing him of not following the instructions. He assured the caller that he had. He was then given instructions to go to a certain address and he would find another note in a tin can. This time the victim's uncle, Mr. Rod Tetcom, followed the kidnappers' instructions to proceed to another place, where he found a note with instructions. He was to drive down the main highway between Seattle and Tacoma, turn onto a certain dirt road, and he would find another note. This note told him to leave the dome light on in his car and walk back towards Seattle. If everything was in order, the boy would be released. He had walked about 100 yards when a man came out of the bushes, took the bag of money and was gone.

George Weyerhaeuser at age nine in 1935, when he was kidnapped off the streets of Tacoma, Washington. (Photograph given to author by Mr. Weyerhaeuser)

On June 1, 1935, the kidnapped victim was found in a shack near Issaquah, Washington. He was unharmed. (Notice how the kidnappers' directions in the Weyerhaeuser case were similar to the instructions given by the kidnapper in the Lindbergh case. These kidnappers may have read the newspapers concerning the Lindbergh kidnapping.)

When George was later interviewed he said he took a shortcut from his school through the tennis courts. There was a man who asked George for some directions, and when he started to tell him, the man picked him up and put him the back seat of a car and threw a blanket over his head. There was another man in the car who had a moustache. He was driven for about an hour. The car stopped, the blanket was removed, and he was given an envelope and told to write his name on the back.

The victim was then blindfolded and was carried about twelve steps, where the man waded across a stream and he heard rushing water. On the other side of the stream he was led by the hand over the countryside for about one-half or three-quarters of a mile. He remembered the ground was uneven and covered with bushes or trees.

The blindfold was removed and George's right wrist and leg were chained and he was placed in a hole in the ground and covered with a board. The two men took turns guarding him until about 10:00pm when one of them said the police might find this hole. George was then taken to a car and placed in the trunk. They drove to another place and while George, still in chains, waited by a tree, they dug another hole and placed the car's back seat cushion in the hole, put George in, gave him a blanket, and covered the hole with a piece of tarpaper.

The FBI learned that on May 26, 1935, the two men, accompanied by a woman, put George again in the trunk and went from Washington into Idaho. There, George was first handcuffed to a tree, then later was taken to a house. He was put in a large closet that held a mattress, two chairs, and a small white table. He did not try to run away because the men told him he would be going home soon. At about 3:30am the next morning the kidnappers told George that his father would soon come to take him home. He was put out of a car on the road and wandered into a nearby farmhouse and announced his identity. The family took him in; he bathed, and was given clean clothes and driven to Tacoma.

George was released unharmed, which meant that if the kidnappers could be located and convicted, there would be no death penalty.

The FBI sent serial number lists of the kidnapping loot to commercial enterprises, banks, hotels, and railway companies. On June 2, 1935, a $20 ransom bill was passed to buy a railway ticket from Hunting, Oregon, to Salt Lake City, Utah. The FBI determined that this purchase was made by Harmon Metz Waley.

Shortly, bills began to appear in discount stores in Salt Lake City. Then police officers were stationed in various discount stores. The cashier in one store notified the officer that a woman who just made a purchase passed a ransom bill. The officer arrested the woman, who proved to be Margaret E. Waley, the wife of Harmon Waley. Margaret was taken to the Salt Lake City FBI office where they determined that she had another ransom bill in her purse. Later that day Harmon was arrested at the place where he was living. After making several false statements, he confessed that he and William Dainard, whom he had met in the Idaho State Prison, had kidnapped the Weyerhaeuser boy.

The FBI determined that the Waleys had burned $3,700 in their stove. Why would they burn some of the money? The bills were not burned so much that the FBI Laboratory could not identify the serial numbers, which were identified as ransom bills. Therefore, if the FBI could identify the serial numbers, so could certain bank employees. At these banks the kidnappers could exchange burned bills for bills not on the ransom list.

Waley had also buried $90,790 which FBI agents recovered on June 11, 1935. Waley said Dainard had cheated him out of $5,000 of the ransom money. (Is not there any honor and fair play among kidnappers? Not only was Dainard a kidnapper, he was also a cheat.) Waley later bought a Ford Roadster that he registered in the name of Herman Von Metz.

The FBI's investigation led agents to the tin cans in which Mr. Weyerhaeuser had found some of the ransom notes. There were fingerprints on the cans and in the shack where George was taken. These fingerprints were later identified as fingerprints of Waley, his wife, Margaret, and Dainard. Waley, Margaret, and Dainard were indicted for the kidnapping of George Weyerhaeuser. Waley entered a plea of guilty and was sentenced to 45 years for the kidnapping and an additional two years for conspiring to kidnap. Margaret entered a plea of not guilty, was tried and found guilty, and sentenced to 20 years in prison.

Now Dainard was still on the loose. On June 9, 1935, Dainard was recognized from a wanted poster by a police officer in Butte, Montana, but evaded an arrest. Later, Dainard's car was found abandoned, and in it was $15,155. The serials numbers matched the ransom money list. In early 1936, bills started showing up in the western part of the country that had altered serial numbers. The FBI Laboratory determined the true serial numbers and discovered they were on the ransom list. Then on March 6, 1936, employees of two different banks where bills were passed made a note of their customer's car license number, which was issued to Bert E. Cole. FBI agents set up surveillance at the address listed for "Cole". On May 7, 1936, FBI agents found a Ford bearing the reported license number. It was in a parking lot enclosed by a wire fence. Later, a man entered the car and tried to start it. It would not start and the man got out and raised the hood. Agents approached him and he was readily identified as Dainard. He did not resist arrest, but the agents removed a .45 caliber automatic pistol concealed in the car. Dainard admitted his part in the kidnapping. The arresting agents recovered $37,374 in the possession of Dainard; the serial numbers matched the ransom list. Agents also recovered $14,000 in $100 bills which Dainard had buried in Utah.

Dainard was removed to Tacoma, Washington, where he entered a plea of guilty on May 9, 1936, and was sentenced to 60 years in prison. He was sent to the U. S. Prison, McNeil Island, Washington. He was transferred to the U. S. Prison, Leavenworth, Kansas. He was later determined to be insane and placed in a hospital.

Further, the FBI determined that Edward Fliss, Dainard's associate, had assisted him in exchanging ransom money. He was located and arrested at the Delmar Hotel in San Francisco. He offered no resistance and admitted his part in exchanging ransom money. He was indicted in Tacoma, Washington, entered a guilty plea and was sentenced to 10 years in prison and fined $5,000. In all, the FBI recovered $157,319 in ransom money or money which had been exchanged for other bills.

Harmon Metz Waley was the last of the subjects in this kidnapping case to be released from prison. He was released on June 3, 1963, at the age of 52.

So, what happened to Waley after he was paroled? Some time later he went to work for the Weyerhaeuser Corporation. I tried to contact Mr. George Weyerhaeuser in Tacoma, Washington, but he was not available. I left my name and number and on March 30, 2006, he graciously returned my call. Almost immediately I knew I was speaking with a gentleman and a man who was courteous and well spoken. Here is a synopsis of what he told me.

He was close to nine-years-old when he was kidnapped. He was closely watched by his captors. He was kept chained and had no opportunity to escape. At one time Waley became discouraged when Dainard failed to return to Spokane when expected and Waley was ready to let him go. When he was finally released, the victim was dropped off on the side of a country road and he found his way to a farmer's house. The farmer drove him toward town, but somehow a newspaper man learned of his release.

The news reporter then "conned" the farmer into turning him, the victim, over to the reporter. It was hard for the victim and his family to get away from the news reporters, locally and nationally, and this notoriety has been going on ever since.

While in prison Waley made contact with the victim's father asking that he be given a favorable recommendation for parole, but his father's death preceded Waley's parole. Later Waley was paroled and wrote the victim, Mr. George Weyerhaeuser, Sr. (now the Chief Executive Officer of the Weyerhaeuser Corporation) asking for a job. The CEO arranged for Waley a job with the company as an equipment operator. The victim saw him a few times while he was working for the company. Waley later left and went to work as an engineer for the Washington State Ferry System.

It could be asked quite appropriately why would the victim, years later, hire his kidnapper? Here is why. The victim felt that Waley deserved to be out of prison after a very long term. Further, Waley spared the victim's life and while he was held captive Waley treated him well. Also, Waley was young at the time and the victim felt compassion for him.

The victim's father never dwelt on the kidnapping with his son nor with others.

When I spoke with Mr. Weyerhaeuser, I told him I was a retired FBI Agent with 25 years service. He then told me that he has a sincere and warm spot in his heart for the FBI. He said the manner in which the FBI handled the kidnapping investigation was a "class act". When he told me this I must say how proud I felt, even more than before, to have been a Special Agent of the FBI. I later wrote to Mr. Weyerhaeuser telling him that when I became an FBI Agent, that it was a fulfillment of many of my hopes and dreams. I also told him that I would like to think that some of the cases I once worked were also a "class act". Perhaps some of them were.

Mr. Weyerhaeuser served in the U. S. Navy when World War II came along; his father had been a soldier during World War I. George Weyerhaeuser went from a kidnap victim to Chairman of the Board of the Weyerhaeuser Corporation, Tacoma, Washington. He is now retired. Mr. Weyerhaeuser, Sr., should have written a book—it would have been a best seller.

# ONE KIDNAPPER KILLS ANOTHER KIDNAPPER

Charles S. Ross, age 72, had retired as President of the George S. Carrington Greeting Card Manufacturing Company, Chicago, Illinois. On September 25, 1937, he and his former secretary and lifelong friend, Miss Florence Freihage, were headed for Grand Avenue just south of the Chicago suburb of Franklin Park. There was a car behind them, which had been following for some time, and displaying unusually bright lights. In a voice that noted he was alarmed, he told Miss Freihage that he did not like the looks of this. He said he was going to pull over and let the car pass. He swung his car over to the side of the road, but the other car veered in front, blocking Ross' car.

A man later identified as John Henry Seadlund jumped out and, with a pistol in his hand, walked to Ross' car and tried to open the door on the driver's side. It was locked and he tapped on the window with his pistol and threatened to shoot Ross if he did not open the door. Ross complied and was forced into the kidnapper's car which was being driven by James Atwood Gray. Seadlund said in a commanding voice, "This is a kidnapping. My boss told me to bring you along."

Freihage protested, explaining that Ross had a weak heart and other ailments. Seadlund asked Freihage whether she was Ross' sweetheart or daughter? No, she said, she was just a friend.

Seadlund pressed the gun against her shoulder and asked how much can he give us—a half of a million—a quarter of a million? She did not know and pleaded that he not take Ross. She offered him the money she had on her. Seadlund took the eighty-five dollars that she had, gave a stern warning not to call the police, then ordered her to lie down while he and Gray drove away with Ross. She complied with the demands until she heard the car drive away into the darkness of the night. She attempted to follow it, but the car quickly outdistanced her. She stopped at the first available telephone and called the police.

Four months went by and Ross was carefully guarded and safely out of reach of any alarm that might have been circulated for the kidnappers. The kidnappers drove into Wisconsin and across into Minnesota where they had a safe place near Emily, Minnesota. Seadlund set in motion a plan to demand a $50,000 ransom. He dictated a letter to Ross, but Ross refused to ask for more than $5,000. Seadlund took the letter from Ross and after reading it, changed the $5,000 to $50,000. He mailed the ransom letter. Later they went to Chicago. The ransom letter was received on September 30, 1937. It was transmitted to Harvey S. Brackett, a former business associate of Ross' at Green Bay, Wisconsin. The letter read as follows:

> *"Dear Dick*
> *I am held for ransom. I have stated that I am worth*
> *$100,000 including the G. S. Carrington Co. stock held in escrow by First National Bank try and raise $50,000*
> > *Yours*
> > *Charles S. Ross*
> *Contact Harvey S. Brackett. Say nothing to anyone except Harvey. All communications will be addressed to Williams Bay"* (A small town in Wisconsin).

The above letter apparently was meant for Ross' wife, as Ross affectionately referred to his wife as "Dick." However, in order to keep the ransom negotiations secret, it was mailed by Seadlund with the following letter addressed to Harvey S. Brackett:

> *"Dear Harvey S. Brackett*
> *Have payment ready on instant notice, to be delivered by employee of Harley Davidson Co. on motorcycle. Road to be designated later Rider to drop bag on highway at signal a shot, or repeated flashes of light. Rider to then continue forward 300 yards and turn off Road on left side. To*

*continue farther would be fatal. Money to be contained in small leather bag of following denominations. 20% payment value in $5.00  50% $10.00 30% in $20.00.  All money to be non consecutive and unmarked and of authentic origin. When ready insert following ad in Chicago Tribune used car for sale dept. Dodge. Good cond. No defect.  (over) amount ready (example $500.00 for $50,000.00 $25.00 for $2,500.00  Name of Rider and address  Harvey you are to hire a motorcycle rider from Harley Davidson Co. and get name and address Say nothing to anyone except Dick. Your friend Charles S. Ross"*

The letter was postmarked September 29, 1937, Savanna, Illinois, and was in the handwriting of Ross. An advertisement was placed in a Chicago newspaper as instructed by the kidnapper.

Seadlund snapped a photograph of Ross holding in front of him the football edition of a Chicago newspaper dated October 2, 1937. In another letter he said that proof of Ross' well-being could be obtained at 230 South Wabash Street in Chicago. This was a camera shop and Seadlund enclosed receipt #10437 where undeveloped film had been dropped off. Also, Seadlund enclosed Ross' membership card for a commercial association, and on the back it had Ross' signature. He also enclosed Ross' automobile registration. Obviously, the kidnappers had planned this criminal act in detail. But they did not plan it well enough to get away with it.

The motorcycle rider left Oak Park, Illinois, at 6:00pm and arrived at a point six miles east of Rockford, Illinois, at 7:50pm. Then a car came up behind the rider and blinked its lights. This was a signal for the rider to throw the money on the side of the road. The rider, according to instructions, ditched his motorcycle about 300 yards from where he dropped the moneybag and proceeded on foot. Seadlund picked up the moneybag and took a circuitous route back to their safe place at Emily, Minnesota. Then the kidnappers split the money, $30,000 for Seadlund and $20,000 for Gray as a co-kidnapper. However, Gray never got to spend any of his money. Seadlund shot and killed Ross and then shot and killed Gray, buried them both in the same grave, and made off with all of the money. Some would conclude that a kidnapper who kills another kidnapper can't be all bad.

Seadlund had met Gray in June 1937 when he picked him up hitchhiking. Gray discovered Seadlund's pistol in the back seat of the car, pulled it on Seadlund, and robbed him of the money he had. Somehow Seadlund overpowered him. Instead of leaving Gray, or shooting him, he ordered Gray to drive the car. Did Seadlund become forgiving of Gray? Apparently so, because they became partners in kidnapping Ross. But they did not become such close friends to prevent Seadlund from killing Gray.

Seadlund buried $36,645 in a typewriter carrying case. He made a fatal mistake when he started passing the bills that had serial numbers recorded. One system he had for passing the bills was at horse racing tracks where there were large crowds. The FBI learned of bills being passed at tracks in the east, the south, and at Santa Anita track near Los Angeles. Under the personal supervision of J. Edgar Hoover, a trap was set for Seadlund at Santa Anita. FBI Agents were behind the ticket sellers posing as "change carriers." One of the bills was spotted, the trap was sprung, and Seadlund was arrested. Was he smart? In planning a kidnapping he was, but not smart enough to avoid being caught.

Seadlund had in his possession $14,512 and part of it included ransom bills. This amount included a winning ticket which paid $18.80. The FBI confiscated his car which was purchased with ransom money.

As a side note J. Edgar Hoover was an avid horse player. He would take two weeks vacation in the summer at Del Mar race track near San Diego, and take two weeks in the winter at Hialeah track near Miami. While in Washington he could be seen at the tracks over in Maryland.

At first, Seadlund denied the kidnapping and murder of Ross, but later confessed. He also led agents to the spot where he hid the $32,645 in a typewriter case. Then he led them to the grave where he buried Ross and Gray.

Seadlund and Gray had planned to kidnap and hold for ransom the St. Louis Cardinals baseball pitcher, Jerome H. "Dizzy" Dean, but decided against it because of the ramifications of being involved with Dean's ball club for a ransom payment.

Seadlund was indicted for the kidnapping and murder of Ross and the murder of Gray. Again pardon the joke, but some would suggest that the murder of Gray should only have been a misdemeanor. Seadlund was convicted and on July 14, 1938, he was strapped down in "Old Sparky" the electric chair, and put to death. He was buried on July 17, 1938, beside the grave of his father in the Klondike Cemetery, a little south of Ironton, Minnesota.

# TWO POLICE OFFICERS CONVICTED

Robert C. Greenlease, Sr. was a wealthy automobile dealer in the Kansas City, Missouri area. He had a son, Robert C. Greenlease, Jr., who was always called Bobby.

On September 28, 1953, at around 10:55am Sister Morand of the French Institute of Notre Dame De Sion, a school for small children in Kansas City, Missouri, answered the door and was confronted by a woman who said she was the aunt of Bobby Greenlease. She said Bobby's mother had just had a heart attack and has been calling for Bobby. The woman appeared visibly upset and the Sister said that she and the others would pray for Mrs. Greenlease. When Sister Morand called Bobby out of his class she did not tell him about his mother's "heart attack".

Sister Morand recalled that Bobby walked directly to the woman and showed no indication that the woman was not his aunt. The woman left with her arm around Bobby and they got into a taxicab. At approximately 11:30am that day Sister Marthanna called the Greenlease home to inquire about Mrs. Greenlease's condition. She spoke to Mrs. Greenlease and learned that she was well and the story the woman told was false. Mrs. Greenlease immediately called her husband who rushed home and, after hearing the story of what happened, called the Chief of Police in Kansas City. The Chief in turn called the FBI.

Willard Creech, a cab driver in Kansas City, told authorities that shortly before 11:00am on Sept. 28th a woman whose description fit the woman who called at the school, entered his cab and he drove her to the school. The woman told him to wait, as she desired to be driven to the Katz Drug Store at Westport and Main Streets. He said the woman re-entered his cab with a small boy fitting the description of Bobby. When Creech last saw them he had stopped and the two disembarked behind a blue 1952 or 1953 Ford sedan bearing Kansas license plates.

Later Mr. and Mrs. Greenlease received the first ransom letter. The letter, mailed special delivery and postmarked 6:00pm on September 28th, demanded $600,000 in 20 and 10 dollar bills, which were to be stuffed in a duffle bag. The kidnappers promised Bobby's safe return in 24 hours, as long as there were no tricks in delivering the money. The second ransom letter, postmarked 9:30pm on September 29th was received, and inside the envelope was a Jerusalem medal. This medal had been worn by Bobby. This letter again demanded $600,000 and stated that Bobby was O.K. but homesick. Altogether, the Greenleases received over half a dozen ransom notes and 15 telephone calls. One of the telephone calls turned out to be a cruel hoax that the kidnapper pulled on Mrs. Greenlease. She told the caller there were two questions she wanted him to ask Bobby. First, ask him who was their driver when they went to Europe last summer. Then ask him what he built in his playroom the last night he was home. "All right" said the kidnapper. However, there was never a call answering these two questions.

The ransom was paid and the kidnappers, later identified as Carl Hall and Bonnie Heady, were rich with $600,000 in cash. The final communication with the kidnappers was a telephone call at 1:00am on October 5th. The kidnappers stated they received the $600,000 ransom money and assured Mr. and Mrs. Greenlease that their son was alive and would be returned to them in 24 hours.

Unknown to the family, the kidnappers had killed Bobby soon after the abduction. He was buried near the house of one of the kidnappers in St. Joseph, Missouri. After the kidnappers had received the money, they traveled 380 miles to St. Louis, Missouri.

On October 5th two metal suitcases were purchased by Hall and the money was transferred from the duffle bag to these two suitcases. Hall took Heady, who was drunk, to an apartment he rented on Arsenal Street in St. Louis. Heady immediately passed out. Carl deserted her after leaving only $2,000 of the $600,000. This proves that this kidnapper was a cheapskate. Don't you agree?

On October 6th, Hall purchased two large garbage bags and a shovel and placed them in a rented car. He drove to Meramec River in St. Louis County where he intended to bury the ransom money; however, he could not find a suitable place. Therefore, Hall returned to the Coral Courts Motel, but he became suspicious of some people at the motel and moved to an apartment in the Townhouse Hotel in St. Louis.

A telephone call was received at the 11th District, St. Louis Police Department, about 3:30pm on October 6th from John Oliver Hager, a driver for the Ace Cab Company in St. Louis. His information led to the arrest of Carl Austin Hall (who identified himself as John James Byrne) by officers of the St. Louis Police Department. His cohort, Bonnie Emily Heady, was soon taken into custody.

Hall was interrogated by FBI Agents and other law enforcement officers several times after his arrest, and he emphatically insisted that practically all of the $600,000 ransom money was in his possession at the time he was arrested by the St. Louis Police Department. Hall admitted the planning of the kidnapping, the actual abduction of the victim, and burying the body in the yard at Heady's residence. He also admitted picking up the ransom money, but denied that he had killed the victim. At this time Hall implicated Tom Marsh, stating he had turned the victim over to Marsh. Hall later admitted Marsh was a fictitious individual and the only persons involved in the kidnapping were Heady and himself. It was not until October 11, 1953, that Hall admitted that he and Heady transported the victim from Kansas City, Missouri, to a point just outside of Kansas City, in Overland Park, Kansas. There, Hall shot the victim to death. He then transported the body approximately 45 miles to St. Joseph, Missouri, where he buried it in Heady's yard.

Heady admitted assisting Hall in the preparation of the ransom letters and notes of instructions to the Greenlease family concerning the payoff of the ransom, as well as going to the school and obtaining custody of the victim using the ruse that his mother was ill.

The boy's body was found by FBI Agents at 8:40am October 7, 1953, buried near the porch of the Heady residence at 1201 South 38th Street, St. Joseph, Missouri. The body had been wrapped in a plastic bag and a large quantity of lime had been poured over the bag. The Greenlease family's dentist identified the body as that of Bobby

Greenlease at 1:05pm on October 7th. Bloodstains were found on the basement floor, on steps in the Heady residence, and on a nylon blouse and fiber rug. There were .38 caliber shell casings also found in the house. These shell casings were examined by the FBI Laboratory and it was found that they had been fired from a .38 caliber snub nose Smith & Wesson revolver that was in Hall's possession at the time of his arrest. The FBI Laboratory also ascertained that a bullet recovered from a rubber floor mat in the Plymouth station wagon owned by Heady was also fired from Hall's .38 caliber revolver.

On October 30, 1953, Carl Hall and Bonnie Heady appeared before Judge Albert L. Reeves in Federal Court in Kansas City, Missouri, at which time they entered pleas of guilty to the indictment of kidnapping and murder. On November 19th, after hearing the evidence, a jury in Federal Court recommended the death penalty after only an hour and eight minutes of deliberations. Fifteen minutes after the verdict was announced, Judge Reeves sentenced both of them to be executed on December 18, 1953. Judge Reeves said, "I think the verdict fits the evidence. It is the most cold-blooded, brutal murder I have ever tried."

Hall and Heady were executed together in Missouri's lethal gas chamber at the State Penitentiary, Jefferson City, Missouri, on December 18, 1953. Hall was pronounced dead at 12:12am and Bonnie Heady was pronounced dead 20 seconds later. I suppose this proves that when two people kidnap and murder together, two people can die together.

Here is the kicker, however: over half of the $600,000 was never found. FBI investigations established that the two suitcases which contained the ransom money, and which were in Hall's possession at the time of his arrest, were not brought to the 11th District Precinct Station as testified by the arresting officers, Lieutenant Louis Ira Shoulders and Patrolman Elmer Dolan.

Both officers were subsequently indicted by a Federal Grand Jury on the charge of perjury. Dolan was convicted on March 31, 1954, and sentenced to two years in prison. Shoulders was convicted on April 15, 1954, and sentenced to three years. Both returned to the St. Louis area after they were released from prison. Shoulders died on May 12, 1962. Dolan received a full pardon from President Lyndon B. Johnson on July 21, 1965.

(As an FBI Agent I was assigned for several years in Las Vegas, Nevada. I once taught a three- day seminar for officers at the Nevada State Prison in Carson City. After the classes, a staff member took me on a tour of the prison. As part of the tour I was shown the execution chamber. The staff officer opened the door and I stepped in. This gas chamber, like Missouri's, had two chairs for condemned persons. I walked around observing some of the facets in the death chamber and then stepped out. Thank goodness I have never had nightmares about this. No, I did not sit down in one of the chairs.)

# *VICTIM* **OLD** ENOUGH TO USE LI STICK

On April 28, 1955, Stephanie Bryan, the 14-year-old daughter of Doctor and Mrs. Charles Bryan, Berkeley, California, was walking home with a friend from Willard Junior High School in Berkeley. She was a beautiful teenager and her mother had recently allowed her to use lipstick.

Stephanie took a short cut through a small wooded area where the treetops covered the path and one could see light at the end, as if one were in a tunnel. When she left the friend she had been walking with, it was the last time she was ever seen alive.

When Stephanie did not arrive home when expected her mother called the police. The police essentially took no action until about three days later, inasmuch as it was not unusual for the police to get reports of a teenager running away. Several days later the parents became frantic and the police did start an investigation. Note that on the day Stephanie went missing, the police department received calls from a total of eight people seeing a man and a woman struggling in a car. This was on the road that one would normally drive from Berkeley to Sacramento. They gave a description of the car and later, when Burton Abbot was identified as a suspect, his car fit that description. A few weeks went by and there was no trace of Stephanie. On May 10, 1955, someone found a French textbook located on the side of the road a few miles out of Berkeley, and the book had been issued to Stephanie Bryan.

This pretty face of Stephanie R. Bryan was shown to tens of thousands of people in newspapers and flyers after she went missing on April 28, 1955 at Berkeley, California. On July 20, 1955 her corpse was found at Wildwood, California by a newspaper reporter after FBI Agents and other law enforcement officers failed to locate a body. Courtesy of FBI.

Georgia Evelyn Abbott, her husband Burton, and son Christopher Wesley Abbott, resided at 1408 San Jose Avenue in Alameda, California. On July 15, 1955, Georgia was searching for a hat in the basement of her home and she made a startling discovery. She searched through several suitcases and boxes without finding the hat. Upon removing the contents from one cardboard box she found a lady's red leather purse at the bottom but did not recognize the purse as her own, and upon opening it she found a red leather wallet. Inside the wallet there was a Willard Junior High School card and other identification in the name of Stephanie Bryan. There she also found a bra, glasses, a school card in the name of Stephanie, other items in her name and a photograph of Stephanie. There were also school library books that had been checked out by Stephanie, and in the purse was an unfinished letter from her to her friend, Theodore "Teddy" Bliss.

Georgia did not immediately recognize the name, which had made headlines for quite sometime in area newspapers, but then she said it "rang a bell" and she called the police. (What Georgia did not know at this time was that her call set in motion a chain of events which would later send her husband to the gas chamber.)

Present in her home at this time was her husband Burton, her mother-in-law Elsie Abbott, and a family friend Otto William Dezman.

Police officers and FBI agents quickly swarmed down on the Abbott residence. While they were searching, Burton sat down and worked a crossword puzzle. At one time he interrupted the investigation by asking if anyone knew the definition of "citation." One officer reported that during this investigation Burton had a very lighthearted attitude and appeared to be attempting to convey the impression that he felt the matter was trivial. When responding to questions Burton laughed quite often.

There was a systematic search made by the police and FBI agents, including the probing and digging of the earthen basement of the Abbott home. They found some books, including a spiral notebook bearing the name of Stephanie Bryan. Also found was a composition book bearing her name. A white brassiere was found and gave evidence of having been torn at approximately the point of joining of the back strap to the cloth.

The officers questioned Georgia and Burton, and Burton informed the officers that on April 28th he was at his fishing cabin in Northern California. However, a witness later advised that Abbott was not there on April 28th, but the next day. He was quite sure of this because he saw Burton on the 29th, the day fishing season opened.

Also questioned by the police and the FBI was Abbott's mother, Elsie Abbott. In the document that I received from the FBI under the provisions of the Freedom of Information Act, there is a document showing an interview with Abbot's mother. Although there were excisions made by the FBI withholding certain information, as is allowed by the FOIA, including the interviewee's name, the FBI made a slip up. Deleted is the name, but in one place "Mrs. Abbott" is not deleted, and it is obvious this person is Abbott's mother as in the document it reads "Mrs. Abbott advised that her son Burton, who she calls Bud...." In this interview she claims that Georgia Abbott "is over-sexed and very demanding." She stated that Burton and his wife had a number of arguments in the past several months and that Burton told her that the reason for the arguments is the fact that Georgia is constantly wanting sexual intercourse and he does not. She stated that Burton told her that because of his illness it is impossible for him to have a sexual relationship.

This is not being placed in this book to add a sexual encounter, or lack of it, but this is very important for this reason: when the body of Stephanie Bryan was discovered and examined, it was determined that she had not been raped.

After Abbott was identified as a suspect, FBI agents and other law enforcement officers went to Abbott's fishing cabin in the wilds of northern California near the crossroads community of Wildwood, west of Red Bluff. The cabin and surroundings were searched; however, they failed to find any sign of Stephanie.

Then a California newspaper reporter, Ed Montgomery, whom I have talked to on the telephone, and his photographer, Bob Bryant, went to Wildwood. On July 20, 1955, they contacted a deputy sheriff who had two bloodhound dogs that he had used to locate missing hunters and also he trained them to locate bears, mountain lions and bobcats. They went to the Abbott cabin and the dogs were released. The dogs started a search in the direction north of the cabin, at which time they crossed the creek, traveling east and south, making a wide circle, and returned to the cabin area. After returning to the cabin area they again traveled north along the creek for approximately 100 yards along the roadway. Then one dog got a scent and started across the road in a westerly direction up a steep slope of a hillside, and the dogs were followed into the thicket where it was noticed what appeared to be a burial of some sort. It was not certain what the dogs had found and it appeared that some hunter had removed the entrails of a deer and buried them, a common practice of hunters in this area. No one touched anything and it appeared that some animal had possibly uncovered and had tried to eat some of the matter, and in doing so had pulled out pieces of material that appeared to be cloth. Some of the earth was carefully removed and a shoe was discovered. Stephanie's body had been found. Burton Abbot was soon charged with and arrested for the kidnapping and murder of Stephanie Randolph Bryan.

The failed search by FBI Agents was a big embarrassment to the Bureau. I can almost guarantee that the FBI Agents involved in the search were censured, suspended for two or three weeks, placed on probation, transferred, or all of these. One thing J. Edgar Hoover would not tolerate was "causing embarrassment to the Bureau." I am sure he personally authorized a press release that appeared in the *Los Angeles Herald Express*. In part it read: "The ingenuity and enterprise of Reporter Ed Montgomery and Photographer Bob Bryant... in locating the body of the victim of a ruthless crime is in the highest tradition of journalism." The article ended with the report that "...FBI agents were unsuccessful in their search."

I have a book entitled The FBI Story by Don Whitehead that I am proud to say is autographed, "To D. L. Smith Best Wishes J. Edgar Hoover." There was also a movie of the same title starring James Stewart. Later I'll pass this book on to one of my grandchildren. The point I am trying to make is that conspicuously absent in this book is the kidnapping of Stephanie Bryan. Why not? I am quite positive this kidnapping is not in Whitehead's book because FBI agents made a search and failed to find the body. Some might suggest this case is not in the book because the book was already in print before the kidnapping occurred. I don't think so. The book I have is a 5$^{th}$ edition with the copyright of 1956. Stephanie was kidnapped on April 28, 1955.

Little one-month-old Peter Weinberger was kidnapped on July 4, 1956, and that tragic story is in Whitehead's book.

Some of the anti-capital punishment buffs have contended that because of the weak, sickly, and frail condition of Abbott, he could not have possibly carried a body, weighing as much as Stephanie's did, up a steep hillside. I agree. However, he got Stephanie into his car did he not?

There was evidence that came out in the criminal trial that microscopic fabrics found, when Burton's car was vacuumed by the police, were the same kind of microscopic fabrics in the clothing on Stephanie's body when it was found. It was also discovered that in Burton's car, other than the driver's door, the window and door knobs had been removed. This prevented anyone at the other three doors from rolling down the windows or opening the doors. Therefore, when he opened the door and took hold of her, could he have not twisted her arm or otherwise marched her up the hillside, and THEN killed her? Of course, he could. I'd like to hear the Abbott was innocent contenders explain this away. Or is it, as it is in most capital cases, there are those who could not care one way or the other about the guilt or innocence of a person, but only that the person should not be executed?

On January 19, 1956, Burton Abbott was put on trial for his life in a California criminal court. There were 106 witnesses who testified and the jury was out six days in deliberations. I would suggest the jury was out six days, not necessarily to determine his guilt or innocence, but as in the Lindbergh kidnapping case, they spent that much time determining his sentence.

The prosecution presented among other evidence the following:

- Microscopic fabrics in Abbott's car matched such fabrics on victim's clothing.
- Those who called police on April 28, 1955, described a car in which they saw a man and woman struggling. This car matched the description of Abbott's car.
- Abbott told investigators he was at his fishing cabin on April 28, 1955. A witness there disputed this contention saying he was not seen on the 28th but the following day. The witness was able to recall this inasmuch as he remembered the opening of fishing season on April 29th.
- FBI agents and other investigators dug up in Abbott's basement Stephanie's French composition book, two books she had checked out from the library the day she went missing, her glasses, two of her school notebooks, and a parakeet book she

bought on April 28. Is burying these items something an innocent man would do? No, he would not.

- On April 29th Burton was at a tavern at Wildwood, California, and consumed a large amount of bourbon whiskey.
- When the victim's body was found her panties were wrapped around her neck.
- Abbott had dirt on his boots that matched the dirt nine inches deep in the grave. Also, a shovel found in Abbott's cabin still had dirt on it that matched the dirt in the grave.
- Human hairs found in Abbott's car matched Stephanie's hair.
- Facial tissue found at the grave matched facial tissue Abbott was using.
- The textbook belonging to Stephanie was found beside the road one would normally take from Alameda to Redding, if one had been going to Wildwood.

One of the police officers who was a witness for the prosecution, blurted out that there were reports of Abbott molesting children. He said this during what has been described as a fiery cross-examination by a defense attorney. I don't know whether or not the judge told the jury to disregard this testimony, but even if he did, if you were on the jury could you totally disregard it? Note that this blurt was brought out by the defense, not the prosecution. Therefore, there were no grounds for a reversal.

As a side note in my career as an FBI Agent I was back several times to the FBI Academy for refresher courses that were called "in-service" training. A distinctive FBI achievement was the establishment of the "Behavioral Science Unit" at the FBI Academy, Quantico, VA. This unit was available to law enforcement agencies throughout the country and what they taught was absolutely amazing. I learned that in cases that were often assumed as rape and murder they were actually murder and rape. One of the Special Agents told us of a case that he profiled. In this particular case, when the body of the victim was found a police officer immediately called the FBI at Quantico. It was suggested to the officer that he have his investigators "stake out" the area where the body was found, and they should find the murderer. They set up surveillance and, in a quiet evening hour, they caught the kidnap murderer when he came back to the corpse. There were also cases where the murderer would visit the grave of a victim and talk to the headstone.

In another murder case the FBI told the local police agency to look for a subject who was frail, had pockmarks on his face, if he had been in the army he probably received a bad conduct discharge, had dropped out of school, and he probably could not hold a job. Further, the police should look for a suspect within a mile radius of where the body was found. The police told the FBI this was simple, the officers would simply check every single house within that mile radius. They did so, and when one set of officers knocked at a certain house a frail looking man with pockmarks on his face answered. The officers told him they wanted to talk to him and he replied that he knew what it was about—they wanted to talk to him about the girl he had murdered.

For a boy like me from Auburndale, Florida, and part of a contingency of FBI Agents that some critics have called a bunch of "law school flunkies" (I was one), this profiling is almost over my head. But it works.

Abbott did not work, he was a student of accounting in college, and received a monthly government check as a result of acquiring tuberculosis while in the army.

His trial began November 7, 1955, and the jury found him guilty on January 19, 1956. The jury made no recommendation for mercy and under California's "Little Lindbergh Kidnapping Law" he was sentenced to death.

Appeals followed Abbott's trial and the California State Supreme Court unanimously affirmed his conviction.

If Abbott's arrest, confinement, prosecution, conviction, and sentence were sources of fear, worry and anxiety, this did not affect his sleep. On the day of his execution he went to sleep at 1:20am and awoke at 5:10am. He asked the guard what time it was, and when he was told the time, he turned over and went back to sleep.

For Abbott's "last meal" he ordered prawns, ravioli, salad and chocolate cake. He saved the cake for later and had a glass of milk with it. The warden asked him how he liked his meal and he replied that it was fine and he enjoyed it.

On March 15, 1957, at 11:25am, Abbott died after nine minutes in a California gas chamber.

It has been reported that the California Governor Goodwin Knight was on the telephone calling Warden Harley Teets. When he got Teets on the telephone he asked had the execution started? Yes it had. Could you stop it? No he could not. The Governor had granted Abbott an hour stay of execution earlier in the day. But he called just about two minutes too late to grant another reprieve.

Did Abbott ever confess or admit the crime for which he was convicted and suffered the ultimate sentence a person could be given? First, what is the difference between confession and admission, or is there a difference? Yes, there is. I was told when I went to law school that in an admission a person does not admit to all of the elements of the crime. For example, a person could be asked did you kidnap this woman? Yes. Did you throw this person's body in the river? Yes. Did you kill this person? No. Whereas in a confession a person admits all of the elements of a crime. Did you kidnap this person? Yes. Did you kill this person? Yes. Did you throw this person's body in the river? Yes.

So what did Abbott do, if anything? I would suggest he made an admission. Note that this is what was reported. On September 21, 1961, a California prison psychiatrist, Dr. David Schmidt, was testifying at San Rafael in a completely unrelated matter. He said that all but about 10 to 15 percent of condemned people involved in widely reported murders, admit their guilt to him. Then he was asked if Burton Abbott had admitted his guilt? He replied that he admitted it, but not directly. He was then asked whether Burton Abbott admitted to murdering the girl in the East Bay?

"Yes," he replied, "indirectly".

What did he mean by indirectly?

He said that under oath he would testify to this, but he would not like for this to get to Abbott's mother. At this point this line of questions and answers was stopped. So did Abbott admit his guilt or did he confess to it? I don't know.

# POL/T/CAL K/DNA||/NG

Jesus de Galindez was born on October 12, 1915, in Madrid, Spain. He was an officer in the Loyalist army during the bloody Spanish Civil War of 1934 to 1936. The Loyalists (Socialists) fought bravely, but finally had to give way to the Rebels (Fascists) led by Francisco Franco. Galindez, like many of his fellow Loyalists, had to get the heck out of Spain. He went to France, then to the Dominican Republic where he had close contact with, and indeed became a close associate of, Generalissimo Rafael L. Trujillo. Then he was for a short time in Cuba. He first came to the United States on March 31, 1946, in New York City.

While in New York City Galindez taught in the Spanish Department at Columbia University, that later awarded him a doctorate degree in his absence. Galindez became an outspoken critic of the Dominican Republic dictator--he had nothing to say that was favorable about Trujillo.

This criticism became so widely known that Trujillo had to do something. But what? A plan was completed, except for one thing. There was a need for a pilot to fly from New York City to the Dominican Republic. This was soon accomplished when an aide to Trujillo was in a nightclub one evening in Miami, Florida, and struck up a conversation with a pilot named Gerald Lester Murphy. Murphy was from Eugene, Oregon. He came from a good family, and in the Boy Scouts he earned the Eagle Scout award. But most important of all, he was a skilled pilot who had been checked out to fly twin-engine aircrafts.

Galindez conducted his classes on the evening of March 12, 1956, and was given a ride to his subway stop by one of his students. Then he disappeared. He was a writer for a Spanish newspaper in New York, and when the editor of this newspaper, and other acquaintances, tried to reach him, they could not. The editor filed a missing person report with the New York City Police Department.

Jesus de Galindez, a Spaniard by birth, was a professor at Columbia University, New York City, and an outspoken critic of the Dictator of the Dominican Republic. He disappeared on March 12, 1956 and never seen again. Courtesy of FBI.

The disappearance of Galindez resulted in widespread publicity. Opponents of Trujillo accused the dictator of being involved in the disappearance of Galindez. In public statements Trujillo denied this and made several remarks about Galindez, including stating that he was a communist.

It is interesting to note that prior to the disappearance of Galindez, the FBI in New York City conducted an investigation regarding the Registration Act (this law required anyone acting as an agent for a foreign power to register with the U. S. Department of Justice). The FBI interviewed the subject of this investigation, Felix Hernandez Marquez. Further, in this investigation they interviewed Galindez. He told the FBI that he suspected Marquez was a Trujillo agent and believed Marques was trying to arrange for his, Galindez's, assassination. Marquez was later interviewed by the FBI in Miami, Florida, and gave an evasive and inconsistent story about his identity and activities. He denied that he was an agent for Trujillo.

Slowly the FBI's investigation turned up information regarding Gerald Lester Murphy. He was born July 21, 1933, at Minot, North Dakota. The family subsequently moved to Eugene, Oregon. Early in his life Murphy became a skilled airplane pilot. However, his eyesight was such that he had to wear glasses, and he could not pass an eye examination to become a pilot for an airlines in the United States. But that did not stop him from pursuing his passion of flying an airplane.

This is how the plot began to unfold: On March 5, 1956, Murphy contacted a firm at Linden Airport, Linden, New Jersey, and told them he was interested in renting an airplane. On March 6th he rented a twin-engine Beechcraft C-18-S, paying $1,500 in cash for the rental. He told the person at Linden Airport that the money came from John Kane (phonetic) who, along with a Mr. John Frank (phonetic) were traveling in the eastern United States. Murphy indicated that he wanted the airplane for a trip to Monte Christi in the Dominican Republic. Murphy later told an FBI confidential source that there was a man who was to be flown there who was an enemy of the Dominican Republic, and that he was being flown there against his will. Another FBI confidential source advised there was a Mr. Kane whom he believed to be a former FBI Agent, or had some connection with the FBI. The FBI showed him a 1941 photograph of John Joseph Frank, and although he could not be positive, he believed Frank was Mr. Kane.

Murphy had checked out the airplane and flown it to a gravel strip on Staten Island, NY. He had installed four 30-gallon fuel drums connected to the fuel system, and then the airplane was flown to the Newark airport. On March 12, 1956, Murphy flew the airplane on a test flight and afterwards he flew it to an airport near Amityville, NY. The FBI developed information that Murphy was going to make a non-stop flight to Miami, Florida. I should reiterate that the FBI received all of this information after the disappearance of Galindez.

At the end of this drama, Murphy's parents furnished to the FBI a flight log that showed he had made entries which were exactly seven days off the dates of the actual flights. Among other entries there was a flight for seven hours and thirty minutes, and it appears the flight actually occurred on March 12, 1956. The log showed Murphy had flown to Monte Christi, Dominican Republic and back.

Getting back to this matter, the FBI interviewed people at the airport near Amityville, NY and a night watchman said that a few days before the big snow storm on St. Patrick's Day, March 17, 1956, there were two people and the pilot who helped a man in a wheelchair into the airplane.

The watchman could give no further information. However, the records at the Tamiami Airport, Miami, Florida, show that a Beechcraft Number 68100 arrived 1:25am on March 13, 1956, piloted by G. L. Murphy. The pilot wanted fuel, but it was unavailable at that hour. The airplane apparently proceeded from Tamiami Airport to Lantana, Florida. An employee there recalls someone at the airport receiving a telephone call from a doctor in the New York area, requesting refueling on the morning of March 13, 1956, at 4:00am. But the plane did not arrive until 5:30am or 6:00 am. An employee filled five tanks inside the cabin located behind the bulkhead.

When the door was opened he observed what appeared to be a person lying on the right side of the plane, and another person seated in the rear of the plane. The person lying down did not move. The pilot paid for the fuel with a $100 bill and tipped with a $10 bill.

After the refueling, ostensibly the plane continued to Monte Cristi, Dominican Republic. Records at Blue Star Aviation Company, Tamiami Airport, show a Twin Beechcraft Number 68100 arrived there in the afternoon of March 13, 1956, and the plane was tied down from then until March 23, 1956. One person talked to the pilot who told him he owned the plane and had been flying businessmen to various places.

The records at Ben McGahey Motors, Miami, Florida revealed that Gerald Lester Murphy purchased a 1956 Custom Royal Dodge convertible on March 16, 1956, and paid $4,412 in cash. Also, a fellow pilot of Murphy's reported that a very short time before Murphy's flight, that Murphy had borrowed a small sum of money. Later, Murphy indicated his financial status had improved remarkably as the result of his flight.

More FBI interviews continued and Murphy's fiancé advised that she last saw Murphy on the afternoon of December 3, 1956, at the airport in Ciudad Trujillo, Dominican Republic. He indicated to her that he had an appointment at the presidential palace with General Espaillat regarding Murphy's desire to sell a special identification card to the Dominican Republic. She later advised that Murphy associated his flight with the Galindez disappearance. He further said that he told Espaillat or Trujillo that he did not want to be a party to such activities nor would he be a party to acts of homicide or larceny. Further, he said he made a recording of what went on in the cabin during the flight of a "cancer patient." He said that he had given the recording to a friend, and if anything happened to him the recording would be released.

Murphy, despite needing glasses and not eligible to become a pilot for an airlines in the United States, was later given a job as a co-pilot for the Dominican Republic Airlines. A pilot with that airlines reported that in a conversation with Murphy, he had in a casual manner asked if Murphy thought anything about the disappearance of Galindez. Murphy said that he did not think, but he knew about it. He questioned Murphy about what he meant and Murphy replied that he could not even tell him what happened.

There were several strange twists and turns in this case and I am not sure what is fact and what is fiction. Reportedly Galindez was delivered alive to Trujillo, who pistol-whipped him and then killed him. But what happened to Murphy who, as a boy, was an Eagle Scout?

He apparently began talking too much about this adventure and he was summoned before Generalissimo Trujillo. He was never heard from again.

What became of Trujillo? He had several mansions throughout the Dominican Republic and would often go to them. The staff at each of these mansions would always prepare a scrumptious meal, and if their dictator dropped in, his meal was there waiting for him. But, what about the other mansions where there was also a meal fit for a king, or should I say for a dictator? What did the servants do with the food? I don't know unless they ate it themselves.

To get to each of these custom homes Trujillo was chauffeured in his limousine. Then some of his enemies got the idea to liquidate their dictator. On May 30,1961, he was riding comfortably when his car was blown to smithereens. Some have accused the U. S. Central Intelligence Agency with arranging this assassination. Was the CIA involved in this assassination? I don't know, but there were those at that time asking where was the CIA when they really needed them.

# A NEEDLE IN A HAYSTACK

On July 4, 1956, Mrs. Betty Weinberger had placed her precious one-month-old son Peter in his carriage. While the child slept she went inside her home in Westbury, New York. She returned and, to her horror, found her son was gone and in his place was a ransom note. In the note the kidnapper apologized for taking her child, but explained that he needed money. He demanded $2,000 (two thousand dollars). I spelled out two thousand dollars in the event someone thought the figure was a mistake. Whoever heard of a kidnapper who demanded only $2,000? Well, there was one in this case.

The kidnapper promised that the baby would be returned the next day "safe and happy". There was a threat to kill the baby at the "first wrong move". Despite the kidnapper's threat to harm the baby, Mrs. Weinberger called the Nassau County Police.

The Lindbergh Kidnap Law had been enacted after the kidnapping of the 20-months old Lindbergh child on March 1, 1932. The law specified that unless there was evidence that a victim had been transported interstate, the FBI and other federal agencies had no jurisdiction until after seven days had expired.

Mr. Morris Weinberger, the child's father, had requested that the newspapers hold off from publishing the story of his son's kidnapping until the next day. All but one newspaper agreed to Mr. Weinberger's request and that was the *New York Daily News*. News reporters swarmed to the drop-off area where the police had left a phony ransom package, but nobody showed up except newspaper reporters.

A letter demanding $2,000 ransom for return of baby, written by "Your baby sitter" to the parents of one-month-old Peter Weinberger who was snatched from his crib on July 4, 1956. The letter was later identified as written by Angelo LaMarco. Courtesy of FBI.

On July 10th the kidnapper made two telephone calls to the Weinberger home with additional information on where to take the money. He did not show up at either place. At the second location police found a blue cloth bag and in it was a handwritten note, apparently from the kidnapper, telling the parents where they could find the child "if everything goes smooth".

Handwriting experts examined this note with the first one and determined they were both written by the same person.

Seven days passed and the FBI entered the case. I have a first cousin, Gerri, who was married to an FBI Agent named Robert D. Simmons and he, among numerous other agents, FBI support employees, and other law enforcement people went to work. The FBI opened a temporary headquarters for this case at Mineola, Long Island, New York. These headquarters were open 24 hours a day, seven days a week. In charge was the Special Agent in Charge of the FBI New York Field Division. The only evidence at that time was that the two kidnap notes were written by the same person. So what were law enforcement officers to do, sit and wait? No. Handwriting experts from the FBI Laboratory, Washington, DC, were sent to Mineola, New York, and gave a crash course in handwriting analysis to FBI agents and other law enforcement personnel.

The investigators were going to examine huge volumes of files in New York State Motor Vehicle Bureau, federal and state offices, schools, aircraft plants, and various municipalities. It was going to be like looking for a needle in a haystack. But this made no difference, the FBI and others came up with a plan: Let's find the needle.

The officers had gone through two million documents looking for handwriting similar to that on the two kidnap notes. Then an agent of the U. S. Probation Office in Brooklyn noted there was a similarity between the kidnap notes and the handwriting of one Angelo LaMarca. How excited this officer must have been. He found the needle!

LaMarca had been arrested by the U.S Treasury Department for bootlegging. He was a taxi dispatcher and truck driver who lived with his wife and two children in Plainview, NY. He lived in a house he could not afford, there were many unpaid bills, and he was being threatened by a loan shark. On July 4, 1956, when LaMarca happened upon the Weinberger home, Mrs. Weinberger was leaving her son and going into the house. On impulse, LaMarca scribbled a ransom note in his truck, grabbed the baby and left the note.

On August 23, 1956, LaMarca was arrested at his home by FBI agents and Nassau County police officers. At first he denied the kidnapping, but when he was confronted with his known handwriting and the handwriting on the two notes, he confessed. He told investigators he went to the first drop site, but was scared away by all of the newspaper people and police in that area.

69

He drove away, abandoned the baby alive in some heavy brush just off a highway exit, and went home. A search was made of the area by the investigators and an FBI agent spotted a diaper pin, and then they found Peter Weinberger. He was dead.

On August 23, 1956, LaMarca was indicted for kidnapping and murder and he was placed on trial for his life. The jury convicted him and did not recommend leniency. After several appeals, including one to the U. S. Supreme Court, Angelo LaMarca was executed at Sing Sing Prison on August 7, 1958.

When it was learned the kidnap victim was not transported interstate, the FBI backed out of the case as there was no federal violation. The law has since been changed and now federal agencies enter kidnappings almost immediately. It should be noted that most kidnappings involve letters sent through the U. S. Mail demanding a ransom. This gives federal agents the investigative authority to get the ball rolling without any delay.

# THE END

# About the Author

Donald L. Smith was born and reared in Auburndale, Florida. He served two years in the U. S. Army as an infantry soldier followed by a mission for The Church of Jesus Christ of Latter-day Saints. He briefly attended the University of Utah and then studied at Oglethorpe University, Chamblee, GA. He graduated from John Marshall Law School, Atlanta, GA in 1959.

In 1960 Don became a Special Agent for the FBI. He served in Oklahoma City, OK; Louisville and Elizabethtown, KY; Las Vegas, NV; and at FBI Headquarters, Washington, DC, where he retired September 1982 after 25 years service.

While in Kentucky he was honored by commissions both as a Kentucky Colonel and as an Honorary Colonel in the Kentucky State Police.

Upon retiring from the FBI, Don went to work for the Pentagon Federal Credit Union in Alexandria, VA, where he set up a security system and supervised its operation. In 1985 he moved to Phoenix, AZ, where he has done investigative work for several companies, managed homeowners associations, and became an investigator for the Air Force doing background checks. He has also worked on this book, one he had always planned to write upon retirement from the FBI.

While living in Kentucky, Don became enamored with the sport of horse racing, and in Arizona has been able to fulfill his dream of owning race horses.

Don has also served on the Deer Valley Planning & Zoning Committee and the Supervisory Committee (auditing) of Credit Union West.

He was a small shareholder in a weekly Florida newspaper (now defunct) and has published articles regarding Arizona Ghost Towns that flourished in the late 1800s.

Now fully retired, Don and his wife, Vera, reside in Phoenix, AZ. They have four children and 19 grandchildren.

www.ingramcontent.com/pod-product-compliance
Lightning Source LLC
Chambersburg PA
CBHW021234280526
45784CB00005B/2101